The Farm in the Green Mountains

The Farm
in the Green Mountains

by
Alice Herdan-Zuckmayer

Translated by
Ida H. Washington
and
Carol E. Washington

Illustrated by Sue Sweterlitsch

The New England Press
Shelburne, Vermont

ISBN 0-933050-46-1
Library of Congress Catalog Card Number: 87-60499
Printed in the United States of America
First English-language Edition
(First published as *Die Farm in den Gruenen Bergen* in 1949.)

For additional copies of this book or a catalog of our
other New England titles, please write:

The New England Press
P.O. Box 575
Shelburne, Vermont 05482

Translators' Acknowledgments

We wish to thank Maria (Winnetou) Zuckmayer-Guttenbrunner, the staff of the Baker Library at Dartmouth College, and the staff of the Baily-Howe Library at the University of Vermont. The author used the following sources, though in most cases the quotations in the original book were not attributed:

Borden, Arnold, and Paul Allen. *Students' Handbook of the Baker Memorial Library at Dartmouth College.* Hanover, N.H., 1930.

Deering, Ferdie. *USDA, Manager of American Agriculture.* Norman: University of Oklahoma Press, 1945.

Goodrich, Nathaniel L. "Dartmouth's New Library." *The Library Journal* (March 1929): pp. 191–94.

Kellogg, Charles E. "What Is Farm Research?" In *USDA Yearbook 1943–1947.*

Quint, Wilder Dwight. *The Story of Dartmouth.* Boston, 1914.

Stimson, Rufus W., and Frank W. Lathrop. *History of Agricultural Education of Less than College Grade in the U.S.* Facts of publication unknown.
Vermont Standard

Contents

About This Book . . . . *vi*

Carl Zuckmayer . . . . *vii*

The Journey to America 3

Backwoods Farm 11

Immigration 20

The Christmases 28

The Telephone 40

The Pet Animals 48

The Beginning 55

The Farm Animals 65

Confusion in the Chicken Yard 77

The Rats 90

Bulletin 1652 99

Life with the USDA 109

Marie 118

The *Standard* 132

Drude 153

The Way to the Library 162

The Library 177

Vox Clamantis in Deserto 188

The Journey to America 200

Epilogue 210

About This Book

This book was not supposed to turn into a book at all. It grew out of a series of letters that I wrote after the end of the war to my husband's parents. They had survived the destruction of their house by fire bombs and were waiting in their old age for our return. Since that kept being delayed, I began to write to them about what had been happening to us in America during the long years of separation. Our existence in these years had, in many ways, taken a quite different form from the circumstances one would imagine for an emigrated writer. Just this life, however, in its primitive, rural setting, had given us a knowledge of and respect for everyday America which many immigrants never get. The more I remembered, the longer my letters grew. After Erich Kästner, then editor of the Munich *Neue Zeitung,* happened to see some of these letters during a visit to the Zuckmayer parents, I was amazed to see them suddenly appear in his magazine section. Encouraged by this and spurred on by many questions, I put together the present account.

Alice Herdan-Zuckmayer

Carl Zuckmayer

Carl Zuckmayer (1896–1977), who appears in this book as "Zuck," the husband of the author, was a leading twentieth-century dramatist and one of Germany's most successful writers of comedy.

After an experimental period in which he served as a theater producer and critic as well as an author, Zuckmayer achieved instant fame in 1925 with his lively comedy, *Der fröhliche Weinberg* (*The Merry Vineyard*), which portrayed the manners and morals of the wine-growers of his native Hesse. Two years later *Schinderhannes,* a play about a nineteenth-century Robin Hood figure, continued his focus on the common people and established him as a folklorist. His best-known play is *Der Hauptmann von Köpenick* (*The Captain of Köpenick,* 1931), in which he expanded a small historical incident into a satire on the German tendency to give blind obedience to anyone in uniform. This play brought threats from the Nazi party, which was then coming into power, and forced Zuckmayer and his family to move from Berlin to their Austrian vacation home in 1933. The arrival of Hitler's armies in Austria in 1938 made it necessary for the Zuckmayers to flee to Switzerland. A year later they emigrated to the United States.

Zuckmayer found his creativity stifled in the writing-factory conditions of Hollywood, and teaching in New York was hardly more congenial. From summer acquaintance with the small village of Barnard in central Vermont, the Zuckmayers decided to turn to farming to support themselves during the war years. They rented a small farm in Barnard and stocked it with poultry and goats. Their plan was to live from the produce of the land and to spend spare time in literary work. The farming was much more demanding than they had anticipated, but the independence of a life close to nature found an answering chord in

Zuckmayer's creative spirit. As a child he had devoured the American Indian tales of Karl May, and he had named his daughter Winnetou after the title character of one of Karl May's books. Walking through the Vermont woods with his dogs, Zuckmayer delighted in encounters with bears and mountain lions, and he found inner peace even in the midst of his anxieties about his homeland.

Only one play came from the Vermont years, *Des Teufels General* (*The Devil's General,* 1946). The plot was inspired by news of the death of Zuckmayer's friend Ernst Udet, who was commander-in-chief of the German air force. Before the war, Udet had confessed to Zuckmayer that he had no use for the Nazis but was such an enthusiastic flyer that he would remain in Germany for the opportunity to fly. The dramatic themes of gradual disillusionment and disgust with Hitler's regime, of factory sabotage, and the hero's final suicide as a test pilot were Zuckmayer's speculative invention, but the reality in the characters, circumstances, and values and the skill with which they were portrayed on the stage won wide acclaim from those who had spent the war years in Germany.

After the war Carl Zuckmayer returned to Europe, where he found a mission in trying to build a new Germany from those positive elements which had survived the horror of the Hitler years. In extensive speaking tours, discussions with German youth, and further dramatic works, his compassion for past failures and hope for the ultimate triumph of good in his homeland were in marked contrast to the tone of most of his literary contemporaries. He died in Switzerland in 1977.

Ida H. Washington

The Farm in the Green Mountains

On lofty meadows—yet by woods surrounded,
You stand secure, though wind and weather blown,
As if you were by heaven only bounded.
You gave me, in America, a home.

With bloodied hands I learned how to attend you:
The fireplace took much heavy wood for heat.
And while moons waxed and waned and were again new,
I lived with spring and tree and animals in peace

Until a new call to the stage returned me
To share the fiery drama of the day.
Yet when in dreams the farm appears before me,
By northern lights back home I find my way.

Carl Zuckmayer

The Journey to America

In May 1939 we received the news that our visas for America were ready for us.

A few days later we received the news that we had been exiled, lock, stock, and barrel, from Germany and Austria. We began to say goodbye.

We had been living for more than a year in Chardonne-sur-Vevey on the Lake of Geneva; we loved the landscape, the village, the vineyards, the house. The hotel owners had become our friends.

We had celebrated Christmas and New Year here, and the golden wedding of our parents.

Now we had to celebrate our departure.

Our parents came once more from Germany, our friends from Austria, Italy, Germany, crossing the border with great difficulty in both directions.

We sensed the approaching war in our bones; we were emigrants; we celebrated our departure as something final and unalterable. We said "Till we see you again" and had only a glimmer of hope of "seeing again."

In all the years in America we longed for Chardonne; you could almost call it homesickness, although we had lived there only one year. For us it was the one place in Europe that was full of untroubled memories.

Our house in Austria, our apartments in Berlin and Vienna had been confiscated, plundered, destroyed — those were nightmares. But we could dream of Chardonne undisturbed, and true nostalgia recalls the unchanged and the changeless.

We came to Barnard, Vermont, for the first time, five weeks after our arrival in America.

The first five weeks after our arrival in New York, we lived in the apartment of a friend whom we had known since 1925 in Berlin. She was in California when we arrived.

We spent five wild, mad weeks in New York; we were constantly invited out, taken to the World's Fair; we saw negroes dance in Harlem, ate spaghetti with the Italians, drank tea in Chinatown, Spanish wine in the Spanish quarter, coffee in Jewish coffee houses, beer at Maxl's in the German section, and ate Wienerschnitzel in an Austrian bistro.

We saw everything, we went everywhere, but never found ourselves. Our friend, who had flown in from California, arrived suddenly and unexpectedly in the midst of this tornado and said, "Let's go to Vermont."

She went on ahead, and three days later she called up to say that she had found a small house for us in Barnard.

A few days later we traveled to Vermont, our first trip on an American train.

That was a surprise.

The train was called an express and took seven hours to cover a distance which it could have covered comfortably in four. It stopped at innumerable stations, stopped with a sharp jolt and started up with equally violent jerks. Only the well-upholstered, velvet-covered seats protected us from broken bones. Sometimes pieces of luggage fell down with the violence of stopping and starting. The passengers laughed and made jokes about it.

That was the first time that we met the slow tempo of America and the friendliness and even temper of the Americans.

It was a hot day, but it was cool in the train.

The air conditioner worked like a heating system in reverse: the windows were hermetically sealed to keep the cold in the cars and the heat out.

It was a strange feeling to be shut in behind windows that could not be opened and, when we got out at the stations (we got off and on at several out of curiosity), to come out of a refrigerator into an oven.

Before our arrival at the stations, a bell began to ring, clear, piercing, and insistent. The bell hung in a little tower over the locomotive, and I could imagine a sexton ringing it, one whose other occupation was shoveling coal. The bell probably comes from the time when it was used on the prairie to drive away herds of buffalo who stood in the way of the train.

After seven hours we arrived a little late. Not at the usual station that we always used later; our friend Dorothy [Dorothy Thompson (1894–1961), American journalist] did not want to meet us there because it is a railroad junction, an ugly town with red brick buildings and the unsettled look that clings to transfer points.

Dorothy was waiting for us at the station with her station wagon, a car that looks like a delivery truck with windows and holds either nine persons or fewer people and more luggage. The luggage can be shoved in through a rear door that opens up. You can also carry schoolchildren, ducks, geese, goats, pigs, and pieces of furniture in it; in short, it is a most useful vehicle for country living.

We drove from the station and the town of Windsor out into the Green Mountains toward Barnard.

The state of Vermont is called the "Green Mountain State." It is surrounded by New York, Massachusetts, and New Hampshire, and borders on Canada in the north.

When I describe the location of the farm where we live to our friends, I say: seven hours by rail from New York, four hours from Boston, three hours from the Canadian border.

Vermont is a small lumbering state with about 350,000 inhabitants in 9,564 square miles. It has great, dense woods and mountains up to 4,000 feet high. Its symbols are the red clover and the hermit thrush. Its capital city is Montpelier, which has only 8,000 inhabitants, and the largest city (Burlington) has a university and 27,000 inhabitants.

The winters are long and unimaginably cold.

The Vermonters raise milk cows: Holsteins, Guernseys, Jerseys, and Ayrshires. They have large chicken and turkey farms. They raise special varieties of seed potatoes, and they have magnificent apples, when those are not spoiled by frost. One of their chief products is maple syrup.

Among the states they are a relatively poor state, but they are not afraid of their poverty; they don't love wealth, they have little to gain and not much to lose. This modesty and this moderation give them an independence from uncertain times and arm them with pride and fearlessness.

We arrived late in the afternoon in Barnard, a little village next to a lake, Silver Lake. Dorothy took us to the house she had rented for us. It was not far from the lake and from the "general store," the one store in the village. A large village common stretched from the house to the graveyard.

When I went into the kitchen and considered how I would manage to start housekeeping in a strange place in a strange land, I opened a cupboard and found everything there — simply everything.

There was salt and pepper, coffee and marmalade; there was everything from shortening, rice, flour, even baking powder, to a jar of pickles, all neatly arranged. Butter, lard, and meat were in the icebox, and as a special "house-warming" Dorothy had put two bottles of Rhine wine from her wine cellar in the icebox. Cigarettes lay on the table in the parlor, there were flowers at the window, wood was piled up neatly next to the stove.

That is not an unusual kind of American hospitality, to fill cupboard and chest for new arrivals and greenhorns with everything they need for a good beginning.

The furnishings were very old-fashioned. The few fine pieces stood in dark corners, while furniture and other things from the nineties were pushed out into the light. Porcelain Dutch girls held books; an open Indian head served as an ashtray; you could hardly see the walls for framed mottoes, heads of presidents, and pretty girls; the furniture was elaborately carved; and there were so many rocking chairs that you could hardly find a solid place to sit. The lampshades were so embroidered or such dark pink that the light spread only gloomily from under them.

The owner of the house, a feeble old lady, was staying with a relative in another town, so I could clear away and store the bric-a-brac that bothered me most.

In the kitchen I found 212 baking pans; with them began my enthusiasm for baking, which has stayed with me ever since.

In this house we spent three months of our first summer in America.

We were dismayed, astonished, and impressed by a lifestyle that was so new and different.

That summer the war broke out in Europe.

The next summer we were in Vermont again.

Autumn, winter, spring lay between the first and the second Vermont summer, only three seasons; to me they felt like ten years.

I can remember little of that time. I only know it was filled with false hopes, lost illusions, self-protection, uprooting, and the fight for existence.

It was the first phase of emigration with all the stages of the impersonal, general fate of the emigrant.

It was the usual course, one had no right to be an exception.

There were the other emigrants: the manager from Bielefeld, who thought he had prospects of a position in a large department store. There was the well-known lawyer from Berlin, who dreamed of an offer to be consultant to a corporation. An extensive practice awaited the famous heart specialist. The writer believed that he had a contract in his pocket which would assure him the production of his play on Broadway. There was the great actor, for whom a career in Hollywood beckoned.

But it all happened differently, quite differently.

The manager was happy when he found piece work, perhaps stuffing dolls for the Christmas market in a factory. The lawyer ran upstairs and down with a box of sausages and sold them mostly to emigrants, because his English was too poor for American customers. The heart specialist sat in a wretched corner somewhere and crammed for his examinations like an undergraduate. The writer — if he was lucky — was retrained in Hollywood. The actor was there, too, waiting nervously for a bit part where his foreign accent could be hidden in the noise of the crowd.

Nothing has changed: America is still the land where immigrants, sometimes even natives, begin as dishwashers, but only very few end up as millionaires. It is a new world, and everything that happened in the old one is forgotten and is not chalked up against you on the big board of the new world, but it isn't written up to your credit, either.

It is called starting from the beginning. "To start all over again" is one of the most meaningful sayings which America has produced.

In Europe it would be "to start from the bottom." The way this worked out was that the plunge was easier to bear for emigrants who had been on top in Europe than for those who had not experienced the "top" in Europe either, and who now desperately tried in wild fantasies of homesickness to make up for what they had missed.

The women were usually the point of stability in the first years of the emigration story. They became cleaning women, or they sold soap and brooms, and in this way they made possible the studies and professional training of the men. Many men felt themselves lowered and insulted by this, and it was a long time before they decided to throw overboard their ballast of prejudices, class feeling, and desire to dominate, and so to lighten the lifeboat significantly.

Yes, it was that. At first it seemed like being in a lifeboat.

The ship on which you had lived had gone under; you floated on the water, had some provisions, and hoped to reach land before a storm. You saw water and sky, but as yet no coastline.

In that first autumn, winter, and spring, our family was scattered to the four winds.

The children attended different schools in different states.

Zuck [Carl Zuckmayer, the author's husband] tried without success to find a gold mine in Hollywood and then took a teaching position at a college in New York.

We found an apartment whose rent was affordable. I kept house and cooked—still an unusual activity for me at that time. The cooking, contrary to expectations, succeeded so well that I thought of developing my skills to apply for work as a temporary cook.

Zuck worked on a book and on much besides that was not marketable. The war smoldered in Europe, and we lived in constant fear of what would happen next.

Zuck had received an advance from an American publisher and had to finish his book as quickly as possible. Therefore we sublet our New York apartment for the summer and rented again in Barnard, and again for three months.

This time it was an old farmhouse, built like a big cabin, which was distinguished by an unusually low rent. It was a strange, old-fashioned farmhouse, lonely, set on a hill above the lake.

Whereas the house in the village had too much furniture, the farmhouse had too little.

Dorothy helped out. She drove up with a truck and brought chairs, tables, curtains, bedspreads. We papered the walls, hung up curtains and pictures. In two days the house was livable.

Water had to be brought from a spring which was three minutes away from the house. Snakes lived by the spring.

Zuck said they were a harmless kind of snake, but I wouldn't fetch water for anything.

There was no plumbing, no bathroom, and a strange toilet in the barn with two seats next to each other, probably so you wouldn't have to be alone at night in the dark.

We used oil lamps and candles and a stove in the middle of the kitchen. The sink was ancient, of black iron, and in the middle was a hole through which the water drained into a pail below. Sometimes the pail overflowed and flooded the kitchen with dirty water.

It was a very old farmhouse with lilac bushes around it and a wonderful view of the lake.

The last owner had had to leave the farm because he was over ninety years old.

Once a neighbor, who sold us her home-baked bread, stopped for a visit.

She went into Zuck's room to collect her money for the bread. She sat down in a rocking chair, began to rock, and talked about the weather and the condition of the roads, and Zuck praised her bread.

Suddenly she stopped speaking and stared at the bed that stood in Zuck's room.

"Oh," she said, "that is the bed in which Mrs. Hawthorn died. I used to visit her often before she died." Then she looked at Zuck. "It doesn't bother you," she said, "to sleep in a bed in which someone died?"

9

"No," said Zuck. "It doesn't bother me. Back home we generally sleep in beds in which people before us have died."

It was a beautiful summer on this farm, and we had many guests.

Once, when there was a full moon, we had unexpected guests late at night.

Dorothy brought a load of friends and her stepson in her station wagon. They were celebrating his twenty-third birthday.

There was a party.

We sang songs in all languages. They understood our songs, we understood their songs.

It was almost dawn, but the moon was still shining, when we found the birthday son sitting on the meadow, cowered down in boundless and complete despair.

They picked him up and drove home with him.

"Strange," I thought then, "that these young people can take so little and get into such hopeless depression."

Three years later, before his twenty-sixth birthday, he fell in France.

At the end of this summer, we took a long walk, Zuck and I.

We went through woods and past many occupied and unoccupied farms.

We had packed our lunch and found an old woodshed where we could eat it. It leaned far to one side, bent from age and snowstorms, and only the wood piled up inside held it from collapse. It was the beginning of autumn and a beautiful day.

Zuck sat leaning against the wooden wall of the shed and smoked his pipe.

I sat munching an apple.

"Would you," said Zuck, "would you like to stay in Vermont?"

"Yes," I said without thinking, "I would."

In that moment I knew that it would work out that way someday.

Later we often passed this woodshed on our way to the next town.

It didn't fall down until the autumn when we went back to Europe.

Backwoods Farm

For three summers we had been summer guests in Barnard. After the third summer we became residents.

We had given up our New York apartment in headlong haste and decided to move to the country. The decision had been made surprisingly fast, but it was no surprise.

In America there are many farmers who come from other professions and have started out as amateur farmers.

The reason for their move to the country is usually that they must reduce their cost of living.

Indeed, in the ill-famed depression years, many families, instead of committing suicide, bought themselves a lifeboat in the country to keep their heads above water, with a couple of chickens, rabbits, a potato and vegetable garden, and that way tried to work at building up their threatened existence again.

We belonged to some extent to those people who could point to a large and serious shipwreck as the cause of their moving, and we wanted to try our hand now as amateur farmers.

Life in the country as such was not an unfamiliar lifestyle for us. We were accustomed in Europe to spending the greatest part of the year, or the whole year, in the country. We did not yet suspect how big an adventure we had let ourselves in for: we had no idea of Vermont winters, and we didn't know what it means to have a farm without adequate help.

In that third year we lived in the same house in Barnard that we had rented in the first year. It was centrally located and gave us more time to look for a farm other than the rustic, but impractical, house on the hill.

First we had to get a car, for in America a car is not a matter of luxury or pleasure, but a necessity.

The nearest small city in which one can shop is nine miles away, the nearest railroad station twenty-four miles, the nearest larger university city twenty-nine miles. Auto salesmen overran our house.

After a week we had bought a splendid Oldsmobile second-hand — that is, used — for $360, of which one-third had to be paid down, the rest divided over sixteen months.

The tax for such a car is eighteen dollars per year, five dollars has to be paid to the state where you live, there is no required insurance, private insurance costs are small, and gasoline is not expensive.

These small costs of keeping it make the auto useful and affordable for a large part of the population.

My new old Oldsmobile held five persons, was painted a distinguished beige outside, and upholstered inside with a gray material that could have been used just as well for a fine men's suit. My Oldsmobile was in no way aged; it was a 1937 model and was only four years old when we bought it, in the best condition, equipped with radio, heater, defroster, cigarette lighter, and an inside light on the dashboard that showed whether we had the headlights on high or low beam.

In this new-bought car of ours I took my driving test and drove that same day on all the highways and byways of Vermont to look for a farm. I saw countless houses and farms in the following days, but there was always something wrong.

Many lay too far from the road, many were set too near the road. I saw little modern houses whose bedrooms and living rooms were the size of beach houses, and whose bathtub, furnace, and toilet were crowded into the same space. Other houses were again larger, but the outside walls were so thin that the wind blew through the walls and moved the curtains.

I saw massive, beautiful, well-furnished houses and longed for the money that one needed to live in them.

And then there were here and there wonderful old farmhouses, half fallen down and often abandoned. They were available for little money, but one would have to spend at least two thousand dollars to make them habitable.

12

These "abandoned farms" are a strange feature of America.

The farms are abandoned, perhaps, because the last owner has died and his heir has a better house. Or a family abandoned the house because they migrated to a more fertile and warmer region in the west.

Often they don't even lock up the house. A couple of chairs, tables, bedsteads remain. The teakettle sits on the stove, and here and there an old piece of clothing is hanging, or an old hat is lying and being slowly eaten away by the mice, and the paper is coming loose from the walls.

If the new owner appears in time to rescue the house from decay, it will generally be his pride and joy. For these abandoned farms have in their basic architecture the material to become beautiful houses.

That was the nature of the houses I saw, and when I came back home again after about ten days, tired and impatient from my fruitless search, I found Zuck sitting in his wingchair, smoking his pipe, and he looked at me mysteriously and with amusement.

Zuck didn't like driving and took long walks daily, six to eight hours through the pathless woods on old Indian trails, leaving the house-hunting to me.

That evening, when I described my fruitless search to him again, gave vent to my discouragement, and called us fools for giving up our good apartment in New York without being able to find the right house in the country, Zuck said suddenly, "I've found the house." He didn't say "a house," he said "the house," and refused to explain further.

The next morning friends came who were also Zuck's publishers.

They decided to go to the house with us.

They wanted to see the house in which we would perhaps live in the future, in which perhaps Zuck would again write. They knew that it was vital for us to find the right house.

They took us to the house in their car. That was a poor idea, since they had a fine city car that was not made for Vermont logging roads.

When we turned from the main road into a woods road — at Zuck's direction — we found a sign. There stood written in a child's hand on a blue arrow: Dream Valley.

The valley was a dream in beauty, and the quiet was broken only by the spinning of the auto wheels in the soft grass, the complaining of the motor, the grinding and rubbing of metal parts on rocks, and the cursing of the driver.

Suddenly the woods opened out and provided an enchanted view. To the right lay meadow pastures, to the left was a little mountain lake with a rowboat. In the distance we could see blue, cone-shaped Mt. Ascutney. And then we saw the roof of a house, a piece of window, and a bit of house wall covered with brown shingles.

The roof, as in many American farmhouses, slopes steeply to the ground floor windows on one side, and on the other it looks pushed up and ends in a gentle slope over the windows of the second story. Seen from the gable end, the roof makes a wide angle, with one side short and flat, while the other falls off long and steep.

The house was locked.

We went around the house and peered in the windows.

There was a bedroom with three windows, wood-paneled walls, and an open fireplace. We were told that this was where the mother of the family had slept.

There was a dining room on the southeast, and over the door hung the motto: "I call to Thee at every hour." On the west side was a living room with six windows and hand-hewn beams on the ceiling. The fireplace in this room consisted in its upper part of one mighty block of stone. How they got that into place is still a mystery to us. Probably they built the house around the fireplace.

In Vermont it was impossible to build for a long time because the great Indian trails went through the land, and on these Indian highways the houses were burned down so rapidly that it was hardly worth building.

The house was built in 1783, after the Indian attacks had to a great extent fallen off. In those days the settlers could build everything, even fireplaces, of stone blocks.

In the large fireplace a teakettle hung from an iron hook. When we looked through the window, it was still gilded, something done by the great-grandchild of the Irish grandmother who had brought her teakettle with her and hung it up there. Later we scraped off the gold, and now it is smoke-blackened as before.

15

In the rocks of the fireplace is a brick oven. A small iron door is opened, straw and wood are placed in the oven and lit, and the stone walls are heated by the fire. Then the hot ashes are pushed to the back, where they fall into the cellar through a small hole and can be removed later. The dough is shoved into the hot oven and baked into bread there.

The kitchen was next to the "living room," as it is called in America, the room where one lives, where the radio and the phonograph stand, where father reads the newspaper, mother sews, and the children romp.

The kitchen was seven yards long and very irregular in width, as I discovered when I had to order linoleum later.

I figured out that I took as many steps in this kitchen in the course of the years as I would have taken to walk to Florida. My family said this estimate was exaggerated, that I could not have gone two thousand miles. They were right, but sometimes exaggeration keeps one from collapse.

Attached to the kitchen was a shed that later became our garage.

Separated from the house was a gigantic barn in which we later kept the hay, the pigs, and sometimes the goats.

Quite near the house stood a little shed in which corn was hung up to dry. It stood on six stone legs like the huts in the Wallis [Switzerland], in which they dry the Wallisian meat. Later I looked at this shed from my bedroom window, and I sometimes wondered whether it wouldn't someday stagger down the steep hill on its six stone legs.

There were five more rooms on the second floor of the house, but we couldn't see them then because we didn't find the ladder.

That was our house.

The Backwoods Farm was its name.

I have often asked painters and architects: What makes a house beautiful, what makes a house pleasant? Can you make a house pleasant purposely and intentionally? How can a planned, well-built house make you uncomfortable, how can a tumbledown farmhouse delight you? It is something indefinable because it doesn't have to do with art directly. A painter explained to me once that it depends on the golden mean, the meeting between geometry and beauty.

16

Zuck sat on the steps in front of the house and spoke about the drawbacks of the house. He knew them because he had been in it the day before.

When he had come near the house, he said, he had seen a man who was mowing the meadow.

"Good weather," the man had said.

"Fine weather," said Zuck.

The man went on mowing, then he laid the scythe down and went into the kitchen.

"Good spring water," he said and came to the kitchen door. "Do you want to try it?"

"Yes," said Zuck.

The water flowed out of a pipe into a tin sink in a thin stream.

The man filled a stoneware jug with water.

As Zuck set down the jug, he said, "I'd like to live here."

"Yeah," said the man.

"Have you ever thought of renting this house?" Zuck asked.

"No," said the man.

"Can we talk about it?" said Zuck.

"Yes," said the man, "come see me anytime."

There was no plumbing in the house, no bathroom, no sewer, no electricity, no telephone, no stoves. The house had not been lived in for twelve years.

How it happened I don't know, but it happened.

We had a discussion with him, the owner of the house, who lived in the next town and owned a store there.

He rented us the house. We didn't really know why he did it, for the rent was low. He was a big, lean, white-haired man, who looked like one of the Pilgrim fathers, stern and silent. He regarded us with a look that we often met later. The look meant: queer, strange, crazy people. We didn't know for a long time that they had considered us odd characters from the beginning.

They, those queer, strange inhabitants of Vermont, could sometimes make life quite difficult for city people from New York, Chicago, or Los Angeles by their mistrust and reserve.

We cannot complain, for we did not have a hard time with them, and that was probably because they thought of us as odd characters.

17

And sometimes I have the suspicion that we did become odd characters in the Vermont air, which hatches odd characters.

The rental contract was contained in the form of a letter, certified by no notary, which gave witness to our mutual agreement: the house owner would make the house livable, and we would live in it.

Then the owner went to work.

That was the beginning of August, and on the fifteenth of September we moved in.

Plumbing, bathroom, sewer, electricity, telephone, and three woodstoves were there.

He, the Owner—we always spoke of him with a capital letter—he did most of the work with a single helper. He got paler and thinner with every day. Zuck worried about it.

"I don't know if He can take it without collapsing," Zuck said, as he saw how He dug the drainage ditch in the stony ground. The deeper He dug, the thinner and paler He got.

We didn't know yet how much a Vermonter can and must take.

Our furniture arrived from New York. There were some good antiques with it, which we had acquired cheaply because the owner could not use these enormous pieces in a small New York apartment.

The great Renaissance cupboard and the chest were set in the living room. The matching long narrow wooden table went into Zuck's room with a Bavarian peasant chest. The twelve-foot-long wooden table, a refectory table from a Swabian monastery, became our dining room table. He, the Owner, brought us beautifully turned church benches, discarded from his Catholic church, which went splendidly with our monastery table.

We also had some solid, modern furniture for our bedrooms. The Owner had left some chairs, tables, and writing desks in the house, and the rest I ordered on the installment plan from Sears and Roebuck, that fabulous mail-order house for everything that one needs in life.

I fell completely under the spell of those Sears and Roebuck catalogs in the next years, and I became an auction follower as well. Auctions in the country are worth going to just for the show, not to mention the real bargains one can find in old handwork.

In that first winter we had as animals only two dogs, three cats, a mentally ill duck, and a feeble chicken. We had been given the duck and the chicken by friends.

In that first winter I had nothing to do but housework, cooking, washing, cleaning, and sewing, especially curtains and bedspreads.

I ordered most of the material from Sears and Roebuck, and since I had no machine, I had to sew everything by hand. Zuck got green curtains in his room, which went well with his bird prints and the pale green peasant chest.

Winnetou, our younger daughter, had white curtains with figures on them: peasants, churches, houses, chests, hearts, trees in red and blue, and from the same material I sewed her covers for the ugly frame of her iron bed that I had acquired at an auction.

Michi, the older, had a room with yellow curtains and pillows on which southern plantation life was pictured. Fine ladies from the glamorous time before the Civil War waved from their carriages to parading soldiers. Black mammies dressed chickens southern style, and in the background were pictured the white mansions of the plantation owners.

We called Michi's room "Gone With the Wind." Perhaps it was a prophecy, for a few years later she married a man from the South and now lives in the southern states.

My room had white batiste curtains, a blue rug, and a chintz-covered down coverlet on the bed and looked like the room of a lady. This I urgently needed as a contrast to working in the kitchen and later in the barn.

The dining room had blue-striped curtains, the kitchen red striped.

For the living room I needed twelve curtains for six windows, and they were made only after Sears and Roebuck had a sale of dark-striped cotton material for men's shirts.

This first winter on the farm could have been very peaceful, if twelve weeks later the war hadn't broken out.

Immigration

That was the house in which I was to live now, and around the house were the meadows, and around the meadows the woods with their uncut underbrush.

There was the pond out of which dead trees stretched their arms like drowning people.

A brook flowed steeply down into a wood in which raccoons climbed up the trees, snuffling porcupines scraped and slid through the bushes. There were sometimes lynxes that crouched with glowing eyes on the rocks and screamed shrilly.

There wildcats spat, there wild rabbits ran, there skunks shuffled and stamped, there a bear sat in the bushes and ate raspberries. In the autumn cranes flew over the woods to the pond, in the summertime hummingbirds whirred in front of the windows, unfamiliar birdsongs came from trees, and in the sheds giant spiders with mighty bodies sat in their webs.

At night the moon stood like a half-lowered sickle over the landscape with its strange animals.

There were mountains wooded with firs, spruce, pine, beech, birch, elm, and maple trees. In the woods there were weasels, martens, and foxes. It was a landscape which resembled the one at home even in details, and yet it was totally unfamiliar and foreign.

It was as if we had come into an enchanted, bewitched wood, in which every shape had been transformed, over which even the moon hung in a different corner.

Even the sky no longer seemed to cover the earth like a bell jar; indeed, it was as if sky and earth had become parallel planes which met only in an infinity we could not see.

This produced a feeling of expanse and boundlessness such as I had never known before.

In optics a sentence about angles reads: "The size of the image on the retina depends on the angle of vision."

Now it appeared that the angle had been displaced and with it the images on the retina.

We could no longer rely on what we had learned before — it was all completely new and completely different.

Many immigrants have experienced and described this condition as a second childhood.

We had to learn again how to see, hear, feel, smell, taste. We had to accustom ourselves to the wide spaces, the division of space, and only very gradually did we find our equilibrium in the unaccustomed dimensions. It smelled different in the woods, in the meadows, in the house.

Everything tasted different, since the earth was sweet and produced sweet plants and fruits. They mixed the sweet with the sour, and the taste was strange to us. We had to learn to talk and to know hundreds of phrases that were needed for daily life. We studied the spoken language, but we had trouble speaking it.

It was all different and completely strange.

In the late fall a loneliness settled around the house, one that came from the outside and thickened until we could almost see it. Later, with the first snow, a stillness fell, a pulsating stillness that swung back and forth and droned in our ears.

It happened Saturday night. Sunday noon Finnish friends called us from the nearest university town.

"What will happen?" said the wife in a troubled tone, "And what are you going to do?"

"What we always do," I answered, unsuspecting, "keep the house warm, cook, clean house, slowly get ready for winter."

"If they let you," she said, and suddenly I noticed that she was speaking English, although we always spoke German with each other.

21

"Has something happened?" I asked.

"Haven't you heard about Pearl Harbor yet?" she asked, astonished.

"No," I said, "we haven't turned the radio on since the day before yesterday. What's Pearl Harbor?"

"The war," she said.

From that hour on we kept the radio tuned in, day and night, with only a few interruptions.

It is a haunting instrument, the radio. There we sat now in our farmhouse, which lay like a Robinson Crusoe island in the woods, and suddenly we heard the noisy sound of human masses assembled in a great room. We heard the scuffing of shoes, the murmur of voices; we heard a group that was waiting for something cough and clear their throats; we heard and saw Washington waiting in our imaginations. Then for the length of one moment a deep, deathlike silence fell, and then he began to speak, "Mister President."

It had been a long, warm, late fall, and we had had only a few cold days, even though it was the beginning of December.

Now, however, in the days of the declaration of war on Japan, a shivering cold began to creep into the house, and we could no longer decide whether it was the external cold or doubt that made us shiver constantly.

We waited three days and three nights to see whether the declaration against Germany would happen.

Monday, Tuesday, Wednesday . . .

We sat imprisoned in a cold damp cave of a mountain, and heard time drip.

"When I return to daylight," I thought, "a hundred years will have passed. Everyone I have known will be dead and everything will be changed."

On Thursday the declaration of war on Germany struck.

Thursday afternoon we found that we had no more provisions in the house, and that we had forgotten to purchase everything from salt to bread.

We decided that Zuck should go to the village store to buy the most necessary items. The round trip to the "general store," the only store in the village, took 1½ hours.

On that afternoon I can recall everything quite clearly and down to the last detail.

I sat in the living room in front of an open cupboard door, on which I had hung a spring coat, and I was sewing the hem of the spring coat. It was a senseless job: I could not use the coat for the next half year, and I don't know why this particular piece of clothing came to hand. Outside the storm howled and moaned like a silk ribbon being pulled through teeth.

Zuck had filled the stove in the living room to the top with large chunks of wood and had built a fire of heavy logs in the fireplace.

In spite of that the cold came in from the outer walls in invisible clouds through the room and chilled fingertips and toes.

Now Zuck stood in front of me with the huge carrying basket on his back and the knapsack in his hand.

"You must not let the fire go out," he said. "I cannot be back in less than two hours."

I sat and sewed on, and suddenly I had a strange, painless feeling that I had a lump of ice behind my forehead, directly above the bridge of my nose. After Zuck left, I abandoned the coat and sat down in front of the fireplace to warm my fingers.

"Now it is over," I thought, "now we are completely cut off from over there. No more letters, no news. Now everything is behind us.

"We have emigrated from there, we no longer belong there. Here we are immigrants, but we don't belong here yet. Will they distrust us here, because we come from the land in which the plague reigns? Will they quarantine us in camps, the way they did in France, or deport us, the way it happened in England?

"This is the end. Emigration and immigration are the same as death and birth. I have not yet been born again."

I sat there, deaf and dumb, and waited for the touch of the witch's staff that could slowly turn one to stone, or for that of the magic wand that could teach one to fly.

When Zuck returned, the fires had burned down and it was ice cold in the house.

Zuck, who did not take it lightly when his fire wasn't watched, was as mild as a philosopher this time, and after only a little scolding got his fires going again.

"What are they saying in town?" I asked him.

"They aren't saying anything," he said, "they aren't talking about the war."

"Perhaps because we are foreigners," I said.

"I don't know," said Zuck thoughtfully, "I have the feeling that even when we're not around and can't hear, nothing is said about the war."

That same evening it happened that, when Zuck turned on the water faucet, only a tiny bit of a blackish, sluggish liquid came out, and then the water stopped flowing.

From the water tank in the kitchen there came a dangerous bubbling, hissing noise.

"There is no more water in the tank," said Zuck, "I'll have to let the stove go out, otherwise the boiler will explode."

I went to the telephone and called the landlord in the village. "There is no more water in the pipes," I said, "and the boiler is ready to explode. Please send someone, or come out to the farm yourself, to see what has happened."

"I'll stop in tomorrow," he said calmly. "I already know you have frozen pipes. They freeze easily at thirty below zero."

We spent half the night working.

Zuck carried glowing coals from the kitchen fire outdoors and hauled buckets of water from the pond, which was covered with a thin layer of ice that had to be chopped away first.

I boiled water in the Irish great-grandmother's teakettle over the open fire in the fireplace and melted cubes from the refrigerator to use as drinking water.

When our landlord appeared the next morning with a plumber, they brought candles, torches, and Bunsen burners, and warmed the pipes with them so energetically and forcefully that a pipe in the bathroom burst. A flash flood poured out directly over our books into the middle of the living room.

All of these catastrophes taught me from that time on to mind the hearth and fire and—no matter what might happen—never to forget to do first things first.

Saturday morning I woke up early, disturbed by a strong white brightness that seemed to shine from the walls of the room.

It was even stiller than usual, and on that morning I heard for the first time that restless quiet which appeared to swing back and forth in thirds like the sound of the cuckoo's call, unrhythmically, often repeating the upper or lower note.

It was still very cold, but during the night snow had fallen, the first snow.

Snowed in, the house appeared to be even more lonely and farther removed from human settlements.

In this snow-loneliness I heard the comforting sounds of the morning. I heard Zuck get up, I heard him lay the fire and go into the kitchen to make breakfast. Between us had grown up a gentleman's agreement that he would be the breakfast cook, and I would be the noon and evening cook, as well as dishwasher. I heard the rattle of dishes, smelled the hot, poured, slowly dripped coffee and began to feel warm, protected, and safe.

Then suddenly I heard footsteps on the path to the house. That was unusual and strange, since in the fall and winter months, after the summer guests and friends had left, almost no one came to the house.

I got up, went to the window, and saw two men climbing the steep hill.

One was in a dark uniform unfamiliar to me, the other was the sheriff of our district.

At first I could scarcely move from fright.

"They're coming to take him away," I thought. "We are three thousand miles from the land of 'taking away,' and now it's going to happen to him here."

I threw on a bathrobe, ran down the stairs, and stopped at the door of the living room.

I could not understand what the men were saying, but their tone of voice sounded calm and deliberate.

"Here are our immigration papers," I heard Zuck say. The interview lasted scarcely ten minutes.

"You will learn all the other regulations in the newspapers," I heard the sheriff say clearly.

Then they took their leave, and I saw them go back down the hill again.

I went to Zuck in the kitchen.

"They weren't able to drive up the hill," he said. "They had to leave their car parked on the main highway. The road is too icy and snowy."

"What did they want, and what else will happen?" I asked.

"Nothing, I believe," he said, "they only wanted to see our papers."

On the same day a snowstorm set in that did not want to stop, and the snow in front of the windows rose like a flood.

During the night we could scarcely sleep.

The timbers moaned and groaned, and often the rafters cracked like dull thuds of cannon balls. That came, as some-one later explained to us, from the large wooden pegs that were loosened in old houses by the storms.

On the following day I opened the kitchen door to go out-doors — it opened in — and the next moment I was standing up to my hips in snow. When Zuck had shoveled me out, and I was back in the kitchen, I said, "We have only two cans left. Do you think that you could get through to the village?"

"I'll try," he said.

He tried it on skis and sank so deep in the soft snow that he took them off again and had to carry them, and they could only be used again on the last piece of the way, on the main highway. He returned three hours later, loaded down like a pack mule, soaked through and exhausted.

After he had swallowed two whiskeys, he said, "That was a lovely expedition. This time it went well. But I must have snowshoes, otherwise it can't be done."

"And we must have provisions," I said, "and not just for a couple of days. We must prepare ourselves here like an Alpine cottage in the Grossglockner [Austria] area. If it goes on like this, we can be snowed in here as long as a week. If only the snowplow would come, so that we would have a passable road again!"

That night the snowplow came.

We fell asleep late, because in this third snowy night a new sound had come: the sliding of the compact masses of snow off the roof and the dull thundering roar of the snow that slid off and piled up in front of the ground floor windows like a glacier. When we finally fell asleep, we were shortly wakened again by an earthquake.

The walls trembled, the windows rattled, the house ap-peared to be shaken to its foundations.

At the same time we heard a motor whining, as though an

26

airplane were caught in a spin, and headlights illuminated our house.

That was the snowplow.

It was three o'clock in the morning.

We quickly pulled on clothes and coats and went down to the kitchen.

The snowplow had driven right up to the kitchen door and had cleared a wide, smooth way.

Now it turned around in the dooryard, rumbling and roaring, so that the back part came to a stop at the kitchen door. It looked like a tired May beetle that had overeaten. Zuck fetched beer from the cellar, and the snowplow men came into the kitchen.

There were three of them. They shook their snow-crusted coats and leather gloves out and hung their wet wool caps up. Now we sat around the warm kitchen stove. They clapped their hands to warm them, and then they drank beer from the bottles.

Then the conversation began. "A lot of snow. It's going to be a long winter. We're coming from Mt. Hunger, where there are a lot of farms. The farms there come first. A lot of snow. It'll get a lot worse yet. It took us two hours from Mt. Hunger to you. It'll last longer. The winter has just begun. Eighteen years ago, that was a winter . . ."

And then came the stories of storms and catastrophes. And suddenly I felt that I belonged to the winter, the storms, the catastrophes.

From the kitchen stove and the three snowplow men a warmth radiated that took away the strangeness for us and lit a spark of hope.

As they got back in the snowplow at 3:30, they waved and shouted, "Good night. Hope it's better for Christmas!" That was ten days before Christmas.

We had forgotten about Christmas.

The Christmases

The last proper Christmas had been in 1937 in our farm-house in Henndorf.

It began with horns from the tower.

Late in the afternoon horns played from the church tower announced Christmas with old songs.

Then the peasant children tramped into our house, thirty-six of them, acted their Christmas play, and were given gifts.

Then came the gifts for the family under the large Christmas tree.

The smaller and younger our children were, the larger the tree had to be.

Then came the meal, abundant and ritual, and then came the staying up until midnight.

We went to mass along the hill to the brightly lit church.

From all sides cloaked figures streamed toward the church, carrying their lanterns in front of them.

In the church a huge crèche had been set up, baroque peasants and shepherds, carved from wood, knelt around the child in the cradle, and in the church itself it smelled of shepherd and peasant worshippers, who knelt in the pews and sang Christmas carols.

After mass we were invited every year by Mr. Carl Mayr, our friend, the hereditary lord and master of Henndorf.

He waited for us in his garden salon. His house looked like a little castle.

The scene on the rare wallpaper of the garden salon was

very lively and portrayed a trip in America with forests, Indians, and coaches in which old-fashioned ladies and gentlemen traveled to Niagara.

There are supposed to be only five copies of this paper in existence, one of them in a house in the state of New Hampshire.

The room itself was full of valuable silk-covered furniture, and there stood the table, festively set with much silver, precious porcelain, and crystal glasses. It held the traditional wake-up meal for mass-goers: weisswurst and beer, cakes, pastry, and wine. Later in the night, champagne. The children remained with us in the room for a while after the meal, then they went back to the kitchen with the housekeeper, who had once been their nursemaid. They were drunk with sleep, but too proud to admit it, and wanted to use and enjoy this permission to stay up late, their longest night of the year, to the very end.

That was Christmas at Henndorf.

It seems to me as long ago as my childhood.

1938 was the first emigration Christmas in Switzerland, a friendly, melancholy Christmas among newly acquired friends at Lake Geneva.

Then followed the first Christmas in America, and it was so very, so completely unlike Christmas that I can only recall it with astonished wonder and a slight chill.

The children spent this first American Christmas in the East, the older one in New York, the younger in her school in Vermont.

We sat in the West, three thousand miles from the children, in an Italian bar in San Francisco, and tried to forget Christmas.

In the windows of the houses stood Christmas trees dotted with colored electric lights that were turned on every evening starting two weeks before Christmas and which gave the impression of a carnival. What appeared colorful and cheerful in San Francisco, however, seemed to be transformed in Hollywood to a haunted sea-bottom landscape.

In Hollywood and the neighboring area, I saw Christmas trees still up on New Year's Day, standing on the streets and in gardens, sprinkled with pale blue lights in the snowless southern landscape and looking like decomposing seaweed around which light-fish had gathered.

By 1940 our Christmas had recovered and improved somewhat.

We had our apartment in New York, the children were with us, and we tried to make the best of our current situation. This is an important American saying, one could almost call it a motto, "To make the best of it."

I had found real colored wax candles with candleholders in the German quarter. Our Christmas tree was dragged back from in front of the window into a corner that lay out of sight of the superintendent and was decorated with wax candles.

On Christmas Eve it smelled of wax and pine, and almost like Christmas.

The use of wax candles on Christmas trees is strictly prohibited in America, although I do not believe that the fire damage in the United States is significantly reduced by this. Especially since it is allowable and common, as a pleasant custom in American houses, to decorate the evening dinner table with pretty colored candles.

Yes, in America the matter of fire and also of house, yard, home, and hearth is so strange and at first so incomprehensible that I have to explain that first to be able to tell about our third Christmas, that Christmas that we celebrated in house, yard, and home, at hearth and fireplace.

The prohibition against genuine Christmas tree candles seems to me a useless attempt to oppose the wave of fires that burn throughout the states and bring immeasurable damage. The casualty list from fires reaches approximately ten thousand deaths a year, and the damages, for the year 1945 for example, amounted to about $484,274,000, or about two billion Swiss francs. In the course of the years I made the astonishing observation that it very rarely had anything to do with arson, yet so little was done toward fire prevention that it is amazing that so many houses and buildings are still standing.

The blame can be laid on a whole pattern of carelessness: chimneys are not cleaned regularly, heaters are not inspected regularly, they let children play with kerosene and woodstoves and let them swing on electric cords, they burn the grass so closely around the houses every year and with so little care that the lightest wind can ignite a prairie fire and lay the houses and homes in ruins and ashes.

And just to look at the ways and habits of cigarette smokers can easily give a person nightmares. For years I used to go to a certain movie house and saw with panicky alarm the cigarette burns of the audience on the seats, the carpet, and the walls.

It was amazing that the cinema only caught fire three years later, and indeed burned down under cover of night, after the last performance, smoldering slowly into ashes and disappearing quietly without loss of life.

For years a strong campaign has been waged in America against fire.

It is aimed at feelings and reason, but it appears that they have forgotten the most important thing: namely to seek the roots that lie in tradition, as it were, in the historical habit of fire.

For centuries Americans have been accustomed to having their houses, scarcely built, laid in ruins and ashes by Indians or other enemies. It was a common, traditional misfortune that forced the Americans to continuous new construction or to further wandering.

Now the respect, the interest in preservation of things, surely has a very close relationship with how much a person has his heart set on things, how painfully he feels their destruction.

Constant destruction appears, however, gradually to deaden the pain, to set aside respect, to loosen ties, and finally to lead to forgetting the past and living for the future.

In the beginning I was horrified at this phenomenon that took place before our eyes again and again.

People furnished a house with unending care and trouble, with the work of their own hands, with vision and imagination. But hardly was the house complete, and they could now enjoy it and take pleasure in it in peace, than they sold it on short notice and looked for another house that they dauntlessly remodeled and furnished with the same zeal as the past house and the countless past houses that they had already left behind them.

I saw American families wander from place to place, move into houses and apartments and abandon them again, in a way that I knew from my childhood memories only in officers of the Austro-Hungarian army, who had to move from Cracow to

Budapest, from garrison to garrison, and who were transferred again and again.

But the American families displace themselves willingly, and always with the hope that the next job will be more pleasant and the next house prettier and better than the one they just left.

Gradually I began to understand the phenomenon: Americans are not dependent on any landscape, any house, any surroundings, because they are at home everywhere in their gigantic and truly borderless land, and for all the differences of the East, South, West, and Midwest, speak one and the same language. They have set up their road signs and information booths across the entire country. Drugstores, gas stations, stores—these can look the same everywhere across the entire wide land and arouse in the foreign traveler the impression that everything is the same in America.

Naturally a place in Texas looks quite different from a place in Vermont, New Orleans in the South has no resemblance to Boston, and one could collect volumes of picture books on the differences in America.

But just for that reason they seem to have set up points where they demand uniformity: the same gas stations for gasoline, the same sandwiches and ice creams in the drugstores, the same things to buy in the chain stores.

Individualism is a private matter in America, but its distribution is much wider and more powerful than one generally imagines.

We had now set ourselves down with infallible instinct in that state which has overdeveloped individualism to eccentricity, that produces odd characters and is woven about by a complete cycle of stories whose main theme is indestructible independence and the will to do things in one's own way, even when the approaches are ever so unconventional.

Vermonters are seen in America as especially whimsical and obstinate and also criticized as narrow-minded and reactionary. I cannot agree with this. I am obstinate myself and measure myself willingly against other respectable obstinate people. Narrow-mindedness I have met much less frequently in Vermont than in Europe, and as for being reactionary, even people who are prejudiced against Vermonters must see that

Vermont has put forward a line of senators and governors who have won a not-inconsiderable reputation throughout the country by their forthrightness and personality.

The old-fashioned things about Vermonters and a certain inclination toward tradition were qualities that eased the transplanting for us significantly.

There were and are around us people and neighbors who incline to a certain stability, and one of the most stable among them is our landlord.

He had indeed, when we rented the house, not been living there for twelve years, because he had a store in town and had had to move to the vicinity of the store.

But in spirit he had never left this house, and he spent his Sundays and holidays, often even a few days of vacation, working in the house and keeping it in condition.

For that reason our first impression of the house had been one of an inhabited uninhabited dwelling. Even then, when it had no running water and no lighting and only a few pieces of furniture scattered through it, it looked like a cared-for and protected house, and we caught on quickly that this involved not simply chance and renting a house, but that this house was being put under our protection and we had to take care of it.

I know scarcely any house that is placed in the right relationship to the landscape like this, and that radiates so much harmony in its proportions, in its simplicity, and in its interior.

We originally wanted to make no new ties; we had a great desire to be as free as the American house changer.

But now there was this house to which we fell victim.

To arrange this house was no art. The furniture moved itself to the places in which it belonged.

Therefore to celebrate Christmas in this house was neither the forced exercise of a tradition or a memory of earlier festivities. It was new and different, and a Christmas that belonged to this house.

Three days before Christmas Zuck had gone into the woods, sought out a lovely fir and cut it down with an axe.

Bringing the huge tree through the snowy woods was not so easy.

When he came into the kitchen with the tree he looked as grumpy as the German Christmas elf, Knecht Ruprecht.

It was, however, not only the weight of the tree that troubled him, but unbearable burdens of uncertainty, unpredictability, probable unhappiness. Yes, I could bring out a whole row of such unfortunate words that begin with the negative and gloomy "un" and that had camped around us in a ring and appeared to glare at us out of all the corners like unfriendly toads and lizards.

One could only hold them at a distance with simple tasks like washing, ironing, cleaning, cooking, sewing—work that led to a definite useful end.

To wash and iron a piece of dirty laundry, to clean, scrub, wax the kitchen floor, to cover holes in stockings with a lattice of threads, to make a wearable garment from whole cloth, or to cook something from all sorts of raw ingredients—that was the same process again and again: namely, going from a disorderly beginning to a state of clean orderliness, or giving form and taste to unformed material.

This endlessly repetitive, primitive process of accomplishment was a greater protection against care, anxiety, and fear for one's life than the application of all manner of understanding, reason, and religion.

This also probably explains the fact that women in threatening and confused times generally find their way more easily and orient themselves less anxiously than men, who are more attached to the chaotic beginning and the stages of development than the final form.

Also, these observations refer more to European men, for America can be compared to a great household where men and women throw themselves into it equally at the beginning, strive madly to reach the goal, and set their minds on the final result.

So I buried myself in those days before Christmas in the timeless and time-consuming business of baking.

Since our Christmas tree decorations had been abandoned in Austria, part and parcel, I bought only a few silver chains, angel's hair, the star for the top, and, most important, cookie cutters. I found hearts, fir trees, rabbits, crescents, stars, and gingerbread men in metal shapes, and now began a nightly baking of Broesel cookie hearts, Linzer cookie trees, chocolate rabbits, nut crescents, cinnamon stars, and gingerbread men, so that the house was enveloped in a cloud of baking smells. I formed marzipan potatoes and rolled Mozart balls. The baked goods lay spread out on fresh wooden boards in all shades of colors to cool, marzipan and chocolate balls to harden their outer shell, while the gilded and silvered nuts hung and dried on strings from the beams of the ceiling.

There was a complete world of shapes and forms collected in the kitchen, and one stood among them firmly.

On the night before the children arrived, I sat in the kitchen and pulled colored threads through the cookies. "Tomorrow you can hang them all on the tree," I said to Zuck, who had always been our tree decorator.

"Are you looking forward to Christmas?" Zuck asked me.

"No," I said, "I cannot look forward to it. I can at best try not to be afraid of it."

We sat and snipped strings and talked about our situation, practically, materialistically, and without illusion.

Foreign bank accounts of aliens were cut off first. Then we had to turn over to the sheriff the splendid big radio that we had been sent as an early Christmas present from an American friend, right after it came, so that the shortwave reception could be removed. We had to swear to have no weapon in the house, which was strange on such an isolated farm. We could not travel without official permission.

They were, all together, not bad or uncomfortable measures, but we could not know if these were only a beginning.

Above all, we didn't know whether the people who were around us would see us as enemies, and there is certainly nothing more threatening than to meet the distrust that arises from misunderstanding and can only be changed into trust with difficulty.

We added up the gloomy facts, we weighed all the possibilities of future misfortunes, we looked for ways out and tried to find solutions. Meanwhile we kept on tying threads, broke many cookies, and ate up the pieces.

On the next day the children came.

Everything was ready, the tree that reached to the ceiling was decorated, and I had only to take care that the children did not nibble the tree away before the evening of December 24.

The children were at that time already quite grown up,

35

fifteen and eighteen years old, but they were to all appearances determined, as they entered their parents' house, to throw a few years away, and during their vacation they acted like bright, lively, twelve-year-old-at-most twins.

They ran through the house, tried to peek through the keyhole into the Christmas room, they called to each other in incomprehensible baby talk, called each other by odd names, and sang the old folksongs and Christmas songs in two parts and with amazing variations.

It was as though we had the whole house full of children. We began to be happy, and we wanted to celebrate for their sakes, in spite of all the uncertain, unknown, and dangerous things that lay outside the boundaries of our house.

Early in the afternoon of Christmas Eve I began to lay the table in the Christmas room.

It was the big refectory table, at which eighteen people could sit comfortably without having to keep their elbows in.

When we had guests, or the children were there, we sat at this large table, but we put no tablecloth on it. Rather, the plates and silverware were put at each place on mats, so that the wood surface of the table remained visible and uncovered for long stretches.

This American style of covering the table not only shows off the lovely wood, it makes it possible also to clean the polished wood surface and the washable placemats after every use, which is cleaner and more esthetically pleasing than the repeated appearance of used and soiled tablecloths.

On that day I took the large damask cloth for twenty-four people that I had inherited from my mother and spread it out on the huge table.

That inherited tablecloth had been rescued at the last moment from seizure by the Gestapo and brought after us into Switzerland with all its twenty-four napkins.

Since we had fled with only the lightest baggage from Germany to Austria and had had to leave everything behind, the tablecloth always aroused a feeling in me as though a cover of a feather comforter or an empty birdcage or some other piece of household equipment torn at random from the closet had been rescued from the enemy and had followed us.

But on that Christmas, as on every following one, this useless piece of baggage received a place of honor, and then lay preserved until the next year in the twilight of the linen closet.

When I had spread the cloth and begun to decorate the table with candles and greenery, I heard something like an auto puffing up toward the house.

It fought its way through the plowed and drifted road and stopped, coughing and wheezing, in front of the house door.

I went to the window and saw a man climb out of the truck whom I recognized immediately, although he had his back turned to me, by his uncommon size and wide shoulders. I went to the kitchen and let the giant in. He wore high boots, ski pants, and a thick wool plaid jacket. From his head he took a cap with turned up side pieces that he could use as earmuffs in a storm.

He looked like a strong, handsome woodsman that daily fells tall trees and in the evening brags about the deeds of the lumberjacks around an open fire and inspires them to new Paul Bunyan feats.

All sorts of stories were told about him, stories that always showed that he was of uncommon strength and would take no kind of affront, even if it was only ordinary teasing, without settling the account with his fists.

They said that he came of a respected family. It was further told that he had fled the city, the people, and his own temper, and had escaped to the country, to farming and solitude, so as to be able to choose his associates here as his own master.

He had three children and also a wife of such charming gentleness that she touched the hearts of the people, and they were accustomed to speak of her as of an enchanted princess who had to live with a powerful giant.

At the beginning I was afraid of him, and above all of his handshake, which was as hearty as it was painful.

Now he stood in the kitchen and stamped his feet the way everyone did when they came in from outside to shake off the snow and ice. In one hand he held his cap, and in the other a great round hatbox for ladies' hats.

He put the hatbox carefully on the table, as though he was putting a heavy beech log on a woodpile in a room in which children were sleeping whom he did not want to wake.

I looked at the box in amazement, then I invited him to sit

down and pulled a chair near the kitchen stove so that the melting streams from his clothes and shoes could run off first onto the linoleum-covered kitchen floor.

"How did you get up here?" I asked him. "The road is almost drifted in again."

"The damn thing goes everywhere," he said, "it goes through everything."

The "damn thing"—a 1915 Ford—stood like an old work horse in front of the kitchen door and continued to snort.

"Shouldn't I put warm water in the radiator?" I asked, concerned.

He stood up, opened the kitchen door, went to the vehicle, took an old horse blanket out and threw it over the hood.

Then he slapped the side of the car as though he were slapping the flanks of his horse.

"That'll do," he said, and then we went into the living room. I called Zuck and the children, who came down from upstairs, and we sat in front of the fire in the fireplace. Zuck threw a large beech log on the fire, and the bark of the yellow beech cracked and disappeared in the fire. Zuck brewed a hot grog to warm up our American, the children and I drank tea with rum, and we talked about the snow, the condition of the roads, and whether one should farm.

Next spring he wanted to start a chicken farm with four thousand chicks; we were thinking of getting ourselves laying hens, ducks, and geese.

"But perhaps I'll be drafted," he said, "then the chicken farm will come to nothing."

Then he stood up and took his leave quickly.

"I must go home," he said.

He went through the kitchen and pointed to the hatbox.

"Our Tu Ulikki made that; she is Finnish," he said. "I hope it's all right."

Then he climbed into his car and started up the motor so that it rattled like a coffee mill.

As he drove away, he waved and called through the broken window of his auto: "Merry Christmas!" and with that he rolled down the hill.

Scarcely was he gone when we pulled the many strings from the hatbox, lifted the lid, and carefully took out one layer of tissue paper after another.

On the bottom of the hatbox lay a ring cake as big as a mill-stone.

I lifted it out and laid it on the kitchen table. It was yellow with saffron, dotted with currants and pistachios, smelled of cardamon, and looked like pictures of Christmas celebrations in Sweden.

We spread ourselves around the cake and spelled out the inscription that traveled over its entire hilly landscape.

There stood written in white sugar frosting and flawless German: "Fröhliche Weihnachten!"

The Telephone

In that first winter we would have learned little about the place and the people if it had not been for the telephone.

With the telephone we could find out how our neighbors were living, what they were thinking, what they were cooking, when they were doing laundry, what was happening to them; from their voices we could tell if they were sad and out-of-sorts or happy and optimistic. We have nine on our line.

That is, we have a party line that we share with eight others. Not the way it is with party lines in European cities, where the signal is a sharp, extended ringing, where a black or white indicator shows that the telephone is now in use and that someone else is on the line without being able to hear him, and you have to wait, grinding your teeth, until the indicator shows that the line is clear. No, we nine are really on one line and share our telephone in the broadest sense.

Recently our telephone company helpfully sent us this notice:

> Sharing a line with others is a friendly custom in New England. Whether they ride the same ski lift [to emphasize this comparison a ski tow line is pictured under the name of the telephone company, to which are clinging two beaming young men, with an even more glowing young woman] or use the same telephone line, everything depends on the friendly New England habit of making the best of a difficult situation. Shortage of materials has restricted the extensive expansion program of the New

England Telephone Company. Soon the necessary materials will again be available, and soon we will again be able to supply private lines for those who request them. Meanwhile, however, we can give telephone service to many who would otherwise not have it by putting more customers on one line. If you keep your conversations short and answer your ring promptly, then you and your neighbors can fully enjoy the advantages of the party line.

Our telephones consist of brown boxes that are firmly attached to the wall and have a black handle on the side. The telephone itself is attached to the box by a wire. We have a modern set, with mouthpiece and receiver in one piece; many, however, still have telephones where you grab the mouthpiece with your left hand and hold it like a bouquet, while you hold the receiver to your ear with your right hand like an earphone for the hard-of-hearing. Each of us has his own ring, a morse code signal which is hard to recognize for newcomers, especially if they are not musical or have no sense of rhythm. Our number is Bethel 69 ring 12. The number 12 is our special signal.

Bethel is the small lumbering town where our central telephone station is; 69 is our line which we share with eight partners. Uninitiated summer guests or strangers from New York ask for our phone with the number 12, but we initiates say our number divided, with the "one" the long tone and the "two" the short tones. Expressed musically, our number consists of a half note and two quarter notes.

We have nine different combinations on our line. Two long two short is the messenger and postman. Five equal rings means the man who has sawdust for our barn. One short one long is the farmer's wife to whom I turn for advice and comfort in difficult times. Two equal rings is a housewife and carpenter's wife to whom I can complain about the weather and fuss about inconveniences. Four equal rings is a frail old lady that we invite to parties and ask about her health. The other partners are not known to us personally, but only by their voices. To learn to distinguish different rings is not difficult. To master your own use of the line takes practice, though, if you want to progress from wretched clumsiness to a certain level of skill. I must honestly admit that it was weeks before I was able to distinguish clearly between two long two short and four equal rings, and the frail old lady who had the four equal rings showed remarkable patience in taking my calls, intended for the postman with two long two short. Sometimes I even reached an entirely unknown party who had the ring one long three short.

It is not that I was especially unmusical. I could sing the signals to myself in the purest tones and the most exact rhythms; I could have played them on the piano or on the harmonica. But to carry that over to the heavy crank on the telephone box—that was the unusual problem. Producing even a ring like one long one short, a combination that sounded like an interrupted melancholy melody—a deep sigh with a short gasp—took me a long time, and the carpenter's wife with two equal rings often helped me by turning her handle in the right pattern for me, because on our line, where we hear all the rings, it makes no difference who turns the crank.

I am glad that I do not know the people with two long one short—that melodic crescendo that breaks off so suddenly. Communication with them would be difficult since they are hard of hearing and their neighbors must often go to them on foot to ask them to pick up their phone when their melancholy signal has been ringing repeatedly, unheard for hours.

When you have reached a certain level of competence in turning the crank on the telephone box, you are also able to interpret correctly the cranking of others. There are the impetuous ones who sound out the long rings like a fanfare and let the short ones follow like accented eighth notes. Then there are the hesitant ones who chirp the long tones and wind up with soft, weak quarter notes. Finally there are the happy ones who let the tones fall in even intervals like cooling raindrops. Even the operator in Bethel, who rings automatically without a hand crank, has her own style, and anyone who has heard the telephone cry its alarm in the middle of the night knows that it is either a matter of accident or death, or someone is calling from Hollywood and has forgotten that the sun sets four hours later there, and that an evening conversation at eight o'clock wakes the sleeper in the East out of his best repose at midnight.

That is then our telephone, a much talked over and versatile instrument that nine partners play.

It is very often busy, but an arrangement has been worked out. You lift the receiver, and if you hear the same persons still talking after a half hour and have the feeling that the important things have been discussed, then you turn the crank. It doesn't ring shrilly in the speakers' ears, but makes a grinding sound when the telephone has been lifted. Then follow the speakers' usual remarks: "I think someone wants our line. Goodbye till later."

We have had to develop a certain division. So I would try, for example, never to call on Sunday after church. Rather I lift the receiver and listen to all the delicious recipes for pies, those delicacies whose flaky melting crusts are a work of art and whose contents, from apples to berries to pumpkins, contain everything you can and can't put in a cake.

At first, when I was a newcomer, I didn't recognize the rings, and often foolishly answered when someone else was wanted; then I withdrew discreetly from the conversation. But when the snow lay very deep around the house and the storm howled and I was afraid that it might take the telephone wires and cut us off from the world, something that not uncommonly occurred, then I felt an irresistible desire to stay in touch with the rest of the world as long as the connection held.

Every conversation on our line can be heard by all the partners on the same line. You can participate silently in the conversations of the others and share their cares, troubles, and joys and thus participate in their lives. A soft click in the line showed that someone had picked up a phone. Generally the audience listened quietly without a sound, but it sometimes happened that someone had to cough or sneeze and thus betrayed his presence. We all knew one of our neighbors by his asthmatic breathing; he was so used to his asthma that he made no effort to hold his breath when he was listening in, and so our conversations were sometimes accompanied by his measured rattling.

This not being alone in a conversation, this telephoning in the midst of an invisible circle, had the disciplinary effect on all of us not to say anything bad about our neighbors and to present for the public a certain friendliness. My own consideration went so far that, when I was talking to German friends, I

said everything unimportant in German, while I translated into English everything significant about the farm, our life, and the weather so that our telephone neighbors could understand it.

Once it even happened that I was forced from the position of passive audience into that of active participant. One Sunday our neighbor with two long two short was called so sharply and insistently that I was sure something had happened and went to the phone. I learned that the farm of the mother of two long two short was burning and our neighbor had to hurry immediately to help. I stayed on the line and could now hear from all eight neighbors, in turn and in stages, the course of the fire, although the burning farm itself was on another line. Now they were taking the cows out of the burning barn, then — there went the floor — the beams were cracking — the roof was on fire — the pumps were working — the barn was burned down — the fire was out — the farmhouse was saved — the barn was insured — all these events were shared by our telephone neighbors. When the fire was out I went back to the kitchen relieved, but then came the signal again, two long two short, over and over, melancholy and worried. I knew that my neighbor could not be back home yet and picked up the phone.

An excited voice insisted that she had rung two long two short and would not let me get in a word. She was calling from town and had heard frightening rumors about the fire. "You don't need to be alarmed," I interrupted her. "The fire is out and the damage was not great."

"Who am I speaking to?" she asked surprised. "Did I get the wrong connection?"

"No," I said, "I am on the same line."

"Are you sure that the fire has been put out? Did they call you directly and tell you?" she asked, still upset.

"No," I repeated, "but I am on the line."

"Oh, of course," she answered relieved. "You are on the same line. Thank you very much for the news."

We nine on the line, we don't want sensational news — we want to hear the everyday things: conversations about recipes, illnesses, weather disasters, weddings, auto accidents, cattle sales, and deaths. Once when a summer guest on our line was involved in suspicion of a poisoning murder and this was discussed in all its details on our line, we laid the receivers down disgusted because this sort of event did not fit our frame of experience.

It is also unacceptable to break the frame and to mix into other people's conversations, as an old farm woman once tried to do. She lives in the wilderness with her brother, who looks like an elf king and is a little feeble-minded. He can neither read nor write, but he understands how to care for the cattle and plow the fields. She (the old farm woman) is a large, strong woman with sharp bright eyes. She wears a dilapidated felt hat and a coon skin that is practically hairless and shows bare leather over wide areas. Her swollen legs are wrapped in rags, and on her feet she wears felt-topped boots. She walks with a cane and tells her brother how to do the work. She looks after the chickens — she loves her chickens and lets her favorites hatch eggs in her bed. Once in a hard winter it happened that she became sick, and her little old brother had to fight his way for hours through the deep snow to the village. Farm women came to help, cared for her and took care of the most necessary things.

The old farm woman got well again and had long forgotten the fright of the illness when Red Cross workers came up to her isolated farmhouse in the spring to lay a telephone line. The town had decided to give her a telephone so that she could telephone for help in case of illness and not have to die alone in the mountains.

The old woman, who had been accustomed to complete isolation for half a century, suddenly had a machine on her wall that connected her with the world from which she had so long been cut off. She didn't understand that this apparatus was intended as a way of giving information. She used it as a way to express herself and audibly joined our circle.

She criticized the recipes, she scolded mothers for using the wrong medicines for different children's illnesses, she told the farmers how to plow and to milk, she mixed into lover's conversations and told them what love could lead to — even though she was an old maid herself, she knew all about snow and ice and rain, she knew better about everything and joined into every conversation. We could no longer say anything — she controlled the whole line. Sometimes it even happened that

46

three or four neighbors joined forces against her, and an exchange of words took place that made a mockery of the idea of the telephone as a means of creating understanding.

In the winter, when the old lady was housebound, her participation in the lives of all of us became more intense, complaints increased, and in the next spring help was sought. Again workers from the Red Cross climbed up to the farm, took the telephone out of the house and fastened it to a tree which stood not far away. Then they built a small booth around the phone to protect it from wind and weather.

The old woman stood at the window of her room and watched what the workers were doing. Then she took an old rusty rifle from the Civil War out of the corner and with it limped out to the tree. "What is this all about?" she asked the workers. "What is the purpose of what you are doing?"

"You may keep the telephone," answered one of the workers, "but here outside you won't want to mix into other people's conversations anymore."

The old woman stood speechless for a moment and stared at the workers. Then she understood what had happened. She lifted the Civil War rifle and struck the telephone booth with the butt over and over again, until it broke from the tree. Then she smashed the telephone that had fallen out of the booth and was lying on the ground. After that she turned the barrel of the gun on the workers.

"You," she screamed, "are not going to teach me what I should do. I don't want your telephone if I can't say what I think; I don't need your telephone if you forbid me to speak. Go to the devil, or . . ."

Since that time it has been quiet again on our line, and fairness and peace are reestablished. We nine are again all hanging onto one ski tow, and we submit ourselves to the friendly old New England custom of making the best of a difficult situation.

The Pet Animals

In Henndorf it was different: Zuck always had dogs there. He lived with the dogs. They were his dogs.

There were two pedigreed dogs, lovely brown spaniels, and later we kept one of their sons.

The female had a litter once a year. Then the house echoed with noisy young spaniels until they were sold or given away. But the original pair always remained, a worthy decoration for the house.

Then Zuck gave me a St. Bernard. That was my dog. He died of poisoning two years later, and afterwards I promised myself never to become attached to or to love another animal.

I succeeded in remaining true to this vow for quite a while. Then in America animals began to besiege me, to force themselves upon me, and to lay claim to ownership by me without my being able to defend myself against them.

A cat was the first.

In our second summer in America, Winnetou came home to spend her school vacation with us in Barnard, and she unpacked a cat.

"I just had to bring her with me," she said.

I shook my head and said, "You know very well that I can't stand cats."

"Yes," said Winnetou, "I know that. But a stupid boy who is allergic to cat hair will be at the school over vacation, and so all the cats had to be sent away."

The exiled cat stayed at our house.

After fourteen days she sneaked into Zuck's dresser, built herself a nest out of his white shirts, and gave birth to five kittens in it.

At the end of the summer, Winnetou packed up the mother cat again. Three of the kittens were given away, but we kept a black-and-white tom and a blonde tricolor and named them Pyramus and Thisbe. Thisbe soon became "Tipsy." It was easier to say and meant "a little drunk."

In the first year of their lives Pyramus and Tipsy produced a single black-and-white kitten. We called it Puss in Boots.

This Boots became the apple of my eye.

At first he took a great deal of my care, because his mother Tipsy, who had nearly died in giving him birth, cared very little for him. In the first three weeks I had to capture Tipsy and force her to nurse, because the difficult birth had made her an unnatural mother. If Pyramus had not been the father, Boots would have grown up as an orphan.

Pyramus, the stately tomcat, groomed, licked, and took care of Boots just like a mother, but at night Boots would snuggle up at the foot of my bed. This arrangement lasted even after he was quite grown.

Boots survived many terrifying and life-threatening kitten diseases, though often professional help had to be summoned. The veterinarian explained that tomcats are always more susceptible than females, and that this was a very weak tom. If he had distemper once more, it would be the end of him.

Through his many illnesses Boots became as self-centered, willful, and spoiled as a child who is often sick, but always gets well again, and can count on the attention and care of those around him.

Meanwhile we moved to the farm. Tipsy lived like a true country cat in the barn and went mouse hunting. Our good Pyramus fell victim to a cat epidemic. Boots, now grown into a 1½-year-old tomcat, lived in the house with us in civilized fashion. He was not wild and detested the free life of country cats.

A transformation happened overnight.

One morning, right after sunrise, Zuck came into my room and stood at the foot of the bed. His face had that purposely blank expression that heralds the announcement of noteworthy and startling news.

I was grumpy about being awakened early, because I had a nearly sleepless night behind me.

Boots had been sick again, and had writhed all night with cramps. I could only relieve his suffering with valerian tea, with the magic touch of my hands, and with old nursery songs.

Finally, just before sunrise, we both fell asleep exhausted.

Now Zuck stood in the room, looking neither at me nor at Boots, and asked softly, "Did you hear the tomcats last night?"

"Of course I heard them," I said. "They fought like tigers under my window all night long and howled like stinking coyotes. Was Tipsy in heat again?"

"No," said Zuck, whispering, with a wary glance at Boots, "no, it wasn't Tipsy."

I gasped. "That just isn't possible," I stammered, looking horrified at Boots.

"But it is," said Zuck. "Boots is a female."

By the next week Boots was quite healthy again, and a few weeks later he bore three kittens.

After that he often had kittens. He competed with his mother Tipsy in bearing offspring. We often had even more cats than mice in the house. However, when Boots was without kittens, was not nursing, and had forgotten his offspring, he behaved himself handsomely, proudly, and calmly as a tomcat, and we were careful not to speak of him as "she."

Boots understood every word that was spoken, and he was aware of everything that happened in the house. He made it clear that he wished to remain the lord and tomcat of the house, and he forced us to regard his periods of motherhood as brief transformations.

He looked at us with his green eyes as big as saucers, penetrating and searching, a gaze that drove fear into many strangers. They thought that the expression of his eyes might someday break out into human language. They spoke of transmigration of souls, and they were afraid of his claws. He became the master wizard of the house, and we obeyed him.

Then the dogs joined the household.

The spaniels had remained in Austria. In spite of the fact that a large Swiss circus had tried to get them, they were not allowed out. They were "confiscated property." Whether they

50

had really been expatriated I was unable to find out later in the records. They were saved from starvation by a woman of Henndorf who had worked for us for many years. She cared for the dogs faithfully and lovingly at her own expense until, one after the other, they died of old age in her arms.

After the loss of his dogs Zuck was not enthusiastic about having others, but we had to get dogs because the property was so isolated, and also because dogs are supposed to provide good protection against large and small predators.

Late in the summer of the year that we came to the farm, our weekly newspaper ran an ad for a good place for two young wolfhounds.

The mother of the young dogs lived with two old ladies in town. The ladies had a lovely house with antique furniture, genuine porcelain, and cut glass. They owned many small dogs that lived in the house, but the wolfhound and her puppies were housed in the garage.

We were watched and questioned by the old ladies to see if we were also dog-lovers. Then we were permitted to choose our two dogs. They were given to us with good wishes, and we could take them home.

They were then just two small, woolly puppies. The veterinarian advised us, for the dogs' and our best interests, to keep them outside like huskies.

They slept in a house built for them and fenced with a wide run so that they could get enough exercise during the day.

Zuck dubbed them Robert and Bertram. We soon had to add a second house to avoid jealousy and strife, since they were both male dogs. Each slept in his own house.

Later, after they were fully grown, Zuck used to go walking with them for hours in the trackless forests, and they would break through the underbrush like huge wolves that had strayed from the pack.

They were not fierce, but they had no sense of their own strength.

For that reason we asked guests not to open the door to the kennel carelessly or when we were not present. Many guests, however, especially the ladies who did not understand about dogs, and boys of an age to want to do naughty tricks, tried it just the same. Scarcely had they opened the catch of the kennel door when the dogs would jump against it, break out, throw the guest to the ground and frolic about him as though someone had given them a new bone to play with. At the joyous barking of the dogs and the shrieks of the guest, we had to rush to help. Picking up and brushing off guests, together with restorative doses of schnapps or cold water, was part of our job as dog owners.

Robert and Bertram, because of their untamed wildness, were not permitted in the house and came no further than the garage, where they slept during nights of snow or ice storms.

One time, however, they did come into the house, and that was on January 1, 1943. Thirty-six glasses stood on the kitchen table, relics of New Years Eve, waiting to be washed.

I stood at the sink with my back to the kitchen door and ran steaming water into the dishpan. Suddenly the kitchen door was slammed open, and two avalanches of snow and ice rushed into the kitchen, overspreading everything.

The crash of glasses and my shrill screams chased the dogs, who had broken into my kitchen like a natural disaster, back out through the open door. But the startling effect of the noise made them turn the kitchen floor into a lake before they left.

In just a few seconds they had smashed all thirty-six glasses to splinters.

When Zuck came into the kitchen a few minutes later, waded through the dogs' puddle, and stood in front of the sea of glass splinters, I was sitting on the kitchen stool and had my soapsuds-covered hands folded peacefully on my apron.

I was as dazed as if I had survived a hurricane.

"I am very glad," I said, "that the glasses hadn't been washed yet."

Then we started cleaning up.

After the dogs joined us, we had the unexpected arrival of the duck Gussy, and with her the hen Elise.

It was in early spring, and we had been invited to lunch with friends.

After the meal we looked around their farm.

In one of the huge modern chicken houses was a chicken that appeared uncommonly miserable, thin, and haggard. It was not being attacked by the other hens, but as soon as it wanted to go to the feeding station they made a game of forcing it away.

"It will die," explained the owner. "It is a healthy chicken, but it can't survive here."

"Can I buy it?" I asked. "I'd like to begin with a difficult chicken so that I can get used to having difficult animals before we get a whole flock."

"You don't need to give me more than fifty cents for it," said the owner. "It doesn't lay eggs because it is too scared. But there is also a duck," he continued, "that you can have for nothing. She is too tough to kill and eat, and she disturbs the entire duck pen." Thus we got to know Gussy, the antisocial duck.

She was sitting on a manure pile as though it was a fortress, angry, solitary, and covered with blood. If other ducks came near, she plunged down from her fortress, ready for an attack. She took on superior forces and retreated after a short time to her manure pile, beaten, pecked by sharp duck beaks and bleeding from many wounds. We took Elise and Gussy with us, packed up in two cardboard cartons.

We built them each a stall in our empty shed, with wire mesh as protection against small predators. There they sat in two birdcages which had enough room to make a cow comfortable.

Elise blossomed. She made up for everything which had been denied her in communal living. After three weeks we had to put her on a diet so that she wouldn't burst.

Later, when the regular farm hens arrived, she held the top position in the chicken house. She was, so to speak, the head-mistress and assigned nests, perches, and feeding spots to the newcomers. She was not intelligent, but her mental capacity fit comfortably in the chicken community.

Gussy's case was quite different.

She considered us her archenemies. She watched us suspiciously and angrily when we brought her feed, as if we might have mixed rat poison into it. But she prospered. Her blood-stained feathers grew smooth and white. Her tough flesh gained firmness and strength.

She made innumerable escape attempts, so that we soon became expert duck catchers. We practiced skills on her that would be of great use later in handling our duck flock.

Gussy taught us that American ducks, especially the Muscovy breed to which Gussy belonged, never in all their lives forget that they are descended from wild ducks.

Later, when wedges of white Muscovy ducks cruised over the roof of our house and plunged into the pond, she lost any resemblance to a house pet or tame duck. On her thirty-second escape attempt Gussy succeeded in getting away from us.

We gave her up for lost, torn to bits by a fox, chewed up by a weasel, murdered by a skunk.

But in early summer, when we already had an impressive chicken yard and some other ducks and geese, Gussy returned.

Where she had found a drake, and where she had laid her eggs and hatched them, we didn't know. It could well have been in one of the fallen-down barns in the woods. But now she came waddling slowly across the meadow, and behind her waddled and chirped eleven newborn yellow ducklings.

She wasn't happy to see us again. She looked at us with the same expression of disgust and dislike with which she had regarded us from the start, but she seemed to have decided to conquer her mistrust to give her young a good place to get food. She did not stay long with her ducklings. She abandoned them when they had scarcely gotten their feathers, turning them over to our protection and returning to the freedom of her wild existence.

Sometimes she came home and lived in the shed with the other ducks. At other times she stayed away for a long time. Sometimes she hatched her eggs in a nest hidden in an old stone wall and then turned her ducklings over to us. We were surprised and had to admire the way she knew how to use the duck pen only as a useful way station, without giving up any of her unlimited wild duck freedom.

In that spring, when we had given Gussy up for lost, we bought a mother duck with two ducklings.

It was a serious purchase. They had neither physical nor psychic defects, and we gave them no names.

At least not at first.

Later we named the mother duck Emma. (Seagulls, too, all look as if they were named Emma.) The daughter died before she could be named, but the son grew into a huge drake. Zuck thought his father must have been an albatross.

The purchase of Emma and her ducklings marked the beginning of real farming. We had started to stock the farm.

54

The Beginning

For twelve years we had lived in Henndorf, surrounded by farms.

Cows grazed under our windows, hens ran across my path, geese and ducks waddled past me. I had drunk milk, eaten butter, my breakfast egg was served up every morning, and yet I had no idea how the animals whose products I ate lived, how they were milked, when they laid eggs, what they ate.

It was not that I had no interest in such matters — it was simply that it had never occurred to me to be concerned about them.

Agriculture, farming: that was a kingdom of its own, a preserve in which you did not trespass if you knew nothing about it.

The specialists, the farmers: they knew, they understood — whether from modern research or from centuries-old heritage — how to cultivate the fields and to care for the cattle.

Inexperienced and untrained persons had nothing to do with these matters.

"The farmer sows. The mower mows. The carpenter builds. The baker bakes. The maid milks."

Those are straightforward simple sentences out of the reader we used as children, and they were connected with pictures that illustrated the activities.

They were bright-colored, attractive pictures. They almost smelled of meadows, hay, wood, and fresh bread. But the activities, the skills themselves, remained foreign to us and

55

incomprehensible. We accepted the sentences and pictures like fairy tales and felt no desire to make them real. And now I had arrived in a country in which there were no fairy tales in the usual sense, a country in which the land preserves are open to everyone who wants to hunt in them, a country in which the hunting areas of life are immeasurable.

I am permitted to sow, to mow, to build, to bake, to milk — I can master everything to a certain extent.

In many areas you will always be a bungler, in others you reach the level of dilettante. A few things you really master and never lose your skill.

First we made an inventory of all the skills we both possessed.

Zuck knew something of zoology, especially about butterflies, predatory animals, and the habits of wild birds — he loved animals. With few exceptions I couldn't stand animals, but I had once studied seven semesters of medicine, including anatomy, and I declared that nothing would scare me — a very important factor in farm life, as it later developed. I knew nothing about animals, but a little about growing vegetables.

How could we acquire our missing knowledge in the quickest way?

We couldn't consult our country neighbors. They lived miles from our house and had plenty of troubles of their own, since a considerable part of their help had been drafted and other farm workers had gone to the factories where they got higher pay.

Servants or maids in the European sense don't exist in America and particularly not in Vermont, where they avoid every kind of serving and subservience. Vermont was not a slave state, so black servants have never been common. Our farm as we planned it would have been much too small for an experienced farm worker, and his wages would have been much too large for us.

We had to get along in the next years with hired boys, who appeared from time to time and then disappeared again. These were half-grown youngsters between twelve and sixteen to whom you had to explain every task.

So it was clear from the start of our farming operation that we were completely on our own and had to travel a theoretical road to practical knowledge and experience.

We had asked ourselves the following questions: What kind of animals did we want to get? Where should we buy the animals? How do you build hen houses and barns? What do you feed the animals? How large would the costs be, and how much the earnings?

Now in America there is the blessed and indispensable Department of Agriculture in Washington, to which I am going to have to devote a whole section. This USDA—that is the abbreviation for United States Department of Agriculture— issues brochures that, in four to eighty pages, answer agricultural questions in clear and simple language.

We learned about this institution through a letter that came in our mailbox one day.

The sender was a congressman, the representative from the state of Vermont. His address was: Congress of the United States, House of Representatives, Washington, D.C.

For the uninitiated it should be mentioned that each of the forty-eight states, whether small or large, sends two senators to Congress in Washington. On the other hand, the number of "representatives" depends on the population, so that a state like California with 6,158,000 inhabitants has twenty representatives, Wisconsin with 3 million inhabitants ten representatives, while Vermont with 361,000 inhabitants has only one representative.

From our single representative I received the following letter: "Dear Friend, Agriculture today is even more important than in the past. The useful brochures listed here present the results of research and experiments which the Department of Agriculture has undertaken. You can indicate on the list the brochures that you would like to have, but it should be no more than five, so that many others can take advantage of my limited supply.

"As your representative in Congress I should like to be of service to you and other Vermonters. Write to me about everything that has to do with legislation, and also anytime you feel that I could be of help to you. Don't forget to include your name and address. With best wishes, Yours, _____"

So we had a representative in Washington to whom I could

turn, and this I did immediately, asking whether I could have more than the usual five brochures sent to me, since I was a layman and a beginner.

To this he answered by return mail that he had informed the USDA of my wishes. "It will probably take some time, but I understand that your order will be sent in a week to ten days," he wrote and concluded, "With all good wishes I remain . . ."

Meanwhile I had learned that the USDA also has branches in every state, and that our branch in Vermont gave out brochures, which applied particularly to the climate and agricultural requirements of the state of Vermont; these I could select and get for myself in the agricultural office in the next town.

In the office one could have ten brochures free, but they gave me many more because I was a beginner and therefore needed a greater number of brochures than experts. In addition the workers in the office encouraged me to ask them the most ignorant and absurd questions without blushing for them or myself.

My choice of brochures dealt with the following topics: The farm budget. How does one select a healthy horse? Mites and lice on poultry. Making butter on the farm. Disinfecting stalls. Caring for milk goats. Raising ducks. Raising geese. Plans for setting up a farm. Pigs. Drying medicinal herbs. Types of chickens. Protection from lightning. Selling eggs. Poultry houses and fixtures. Dairying for beginners. The farm garden. Keeping gasoline and kerosene on the farm. Choosing hens for egg production. Working clothes for women. White ladino clover. Types of potatoes on Vermont farms. How to serve maple syrup on snow. How to make a good manure pile. Animals for the small farm. Feeding chickens. Currants and gooseberries and their relationship to rust infection in white pines. Sale of farm products by mail. Making slipcovers for armchairs.

For Zuck I got: The life of wild birds on the farm pond. Taking care of fireplaces and stoves. A dry cellar. Sharpening knives.

There were two brochures that I had ordered only for historic-economic reasons which I didn't receive — Vermont laws which affect home and family, and financial agreements between father and son on the farm — probably because the

58

inquiry about them was so small that they were no longer printed.

All winter we studied, discussed, estimated, and considered brochures.

First we thought of getting hens, ducks, geese, pigs, cows, and horses.

We gave up the cows and horses. Our calculations showed that cows — even if there were only two of them — would require costly remodeling of the present barns, a considerable purchase of equipment for the production of milk and butter, and that transporting the milk to a collection point on a road that was almost impassable for about six months of the year would be an unsolvable problem. For our own use the milk products made little sense — butter takes a lot of work, and the whole family except me detested milk.

When Michi, my oldest daughter, at the ripe age of twenty-one suddenly began to drink a glass of milk every evening about six o'clock, I couldn't understand what had caused this change of heart — until I happened to take a sip from her glass and realized that a healthy shot of whiskey had changed the milk into a cocktail. Instead of cows we decided to get goats, which were more satisfactory animals in every way and offered many advantages.

Horses were also struck from the list, although Zuck and Winnetou are enthusiastic riders, but we could not afford riding horses. Also in "Animals for the Small Farm" I found the deciding sentence: "Even if a horse or a tractor would appear to be necessary for plowing, it is much more advantageous for the owner of a small farm to hire this kind of help than to buy a horse for it and to feed him. However, if the small farmer wants to hire himself out to his neighbors from time to time for plowing and cultivating their fields, the purchase of a horse to use this way could be justified." Zuck and Winnetou did not want to hire themselves out to the neighbors from time to time, so they got no horse. Rather we sometimes hired neighbors, who plowed and harrowed with oxen or horses because our land was too hilly for tractors.

When we had decided on the variety and type of animals, we went bravely ahead to build outbuildings.

It was a good thing that we didn't know all the problems and troubles that we would have with them.

Early in May when the worst frost was past, we began with the construction of chicken houses and the remodeling of the old barns.

I went to a carpenter, a careful older man. He checked the plans, evaluated them, and ordered the wood and the roofing. I was to buy the nails, the windows, and the fixtures.

When all the materials were together, the carpenter did not appear at first, for all good things take time, and it is unacceptable to push for work and pay in Vermont.

After a week of impatient waiting, we found a little note in our mail which said: "Could not come. Was very busy. Haven't forgotten you. Coming Saturday."

He came and worked quite alone. Zuck held the heavy foundation beams for him, and sometimes I was allowed to hold nails and to look for misplaced tools.

I had never before taken part in the day-by-day and hour-by-hour construction of a house, and since in America it is all right to ask questions, I asked my expert carpenter one after another.

Each time, before he answered one of my questions, he stopped working and squatted down — whether he was balancing on a roof rafter or standing on the ladder — pushed his spectacles down almost to his mouth, gave me a searching look, and then explained everything I had asked understandably and wisely through his spectacles while he moved them gently with his lips.

Meanwhile another man worked on the construction of goat and pig stalls in an existing barn. There was nothing leisurely about him.

He was called "Wodan" because he was missing an eye, and his hair fell down wildly over that side.

He came racing up the mountain in his truck and took the curve around the house in a way that made us afraid that a corner of the house would be taken off.

He roared like a hurricane over the house.

Once, when he was roofing our house, the old shingles rattled down in our vegetable garden like hailstones. He tore young birches out of the earth roots and all to use for fence posts, and he mixed cement like an angry demon.

60

The story was told about him that he could eat sixteen servings of ice cream and drink beer on top of that without bursting. He was the Paul Bunyan of the East, a match for the legendary giant woodcutter of the West who can do anything.

At first he couldn't stand us and grumbled: why the devil had these damned foreigners found themselves such a cursed spot, when they would have done better to go to the city.

Gradually I learned to understand his cursing. One day, however, when he stamped across my freshly washed kitchen floor with his gigantic shoes covered with manure, cement, and lime, I blew up, and from that time on we became friends. After that our conversations took on an honest, open form, and I used to say to him clearly, "Fix the roof, but perhaps you should try not to break off the chimney and throw it through my kitchen window."

Or I would say to him, "Clean up the pond, but be careful that you don't send the overflow through our house — I don't like trout in the living room."

He remained a veritable Niagara, but with time we managed to channel him somewhat with a few dams.

Sometimes he brought his wife with him.

She stayed in the truck and would not come into the house, and she read. She was dressed elegantly; her hair and fingernails were beautifully cared for, and she always read the latest works of American literature.

Wodan used to put a cushion behind his wife's back before he started work, and this leather pillow at her back made her posture even more severe and formal.

On those days Wodan worked quietly and behaved like an eagle with clipped wings.

In four weeks the stalls were done.

The most splendid buildings were the brand-new chicken houses, which stood two hundred feet from the house in the middle of lovely fields and hills, and from whose windows you had a beautiful view of the mountains. I must confess that I secretly played with the idea of moving into the new outbuildings instead of the chickens, and leaving the big house to the children and guests, but we soberly resisted the temptation.

The chicken houses stood on enormous stones, so that if we should ever want to move them and set them on another place, we just needed to replace the stone feet with wheels and so turn a chicken house into a circus wagon that could be pulled by horses or tractors. The chicken houses were built according to all the rules developed from collective experience (not ours but the USDA's). The windows were on the south. They were casement windows that could be opened and shut. They were equipped with screens, and over each was a ventilation flap. The window wall was seven feet high, but the opposite wall only five feet, so that the roof fell off steeply from the front wall to slide the snow off in winter. We often forgot the steep ceiling when we were cleaning the hen houses and bumped our heads so that we fell, saw stars, and looked like the knocked-out prize fighter who sinks to his knees in a film.

On the back wall was a kind of large, open drawer with perches over it where the chickens sat and slept at night.

Three times a week we could conveniently and quickly gather the considerable supply of chicken manure from the drawer with a broom and shovel, take it away, and deposit it on our future compost heap.

On the side wall across from the door were hung the nests. They were sent already assembled from Sears and Roebuck and looked like little tin houses, with ten round openings, five in the first floor and five in the second floor, and in front of each a perch on which the hens could walk and look for a nest to lay their eggs. The nests had to stand about twenty inches off the floor, because hens want to jump or flutter up to take care of every important piece of business in their lives, probably in memory of their inheritance from the bird world.

Once, when the wall hooks had become loose and had to be repaired, we placed the laying nests on the floor for two days. During the entire time, the ground floor nests remained unused, while the hens argued and fought over the nests on the second floor.

The long feed troughs in the middle of the chicken houses also stood on iron feet. They looked like the tables and benches in forest cafes or in front of mountain huts: in the middle was the long feed trough, to the right and left of it were two narrow boards on which the chickens could sit for eating. The feed trough was covered with iron bars through which the chickens could stick their heads. Without these bars they loved to walk up and down in their feed, to scratch in it and to dirty it.

The floors of the houses were covered with sawdust. We added some hay to the sawdust in the nests—although hay was not really prescribed—but the chickens obviously liked it.

Then there were drinking water containers, little tanks with floats that lay on the water like a ring and kept the water in the bowl at a certain level.

Providing water for the poultry was difficult on hot summer days, since we had no water pipes to the chicken houses and had to carry the water from our house. But in winter, providing water for the animals became one of the most horrible plagues and catastrophes in our farm experience.

When the chicken houses and stalls were done, I waited for the arrival of Winnetou, who was coming home for spring vacation, to go with me to get the animals we had ordered.

First we got six full-grown hens from a farm. They were light gray striped with black and looked like giant guinea fowl.

The day when the first six arrived was a fine warm day. The sun shone through the sparkling windowpanes of the chicken houses. The sawdust smelled of fresh-cut wood, and the hay gave its fragrance from the nests.

Elise the hen looked over the chicken house and decided that the feed for seven was there for her alone.

Then we carried the boxes in which we had transported the chickens into the chicken house and opened the cage doors and waited. The chickens walked one after another out of the cages and surveyed their new home quietly and without excitement.

Elise did not let their arrival disturb her eating, and the six newcomers soon hopped up on the shelf to enjoy their clean fresh food too.

Winnetou and I stood for half the day at the window and watched our first chickens as they scratched, ate, and picked up grains of corn.

It even happened that a hen looked for a nest and began to lay an egg, an unusual event when you think that chickens sometimes need from three days to a week to recover from the shock of moving and to return to the habit of laying eggs.

Soon we could tell the six hens apart by their feathers, their movements, and their facial expressions. "They are the founders of our flock," said Winnetou, and we named them:

Michaela, Maria, Magdalena, Christina, Augusta, Agatha. All these names came from the rich treasure of names that our daughters had been given.

A week later we had all the animals together: fifty-seven chickens, twenty ducks, five geese, four goats, two pigs, two dogs, and three cats. With these ninety-three animals our farm life began. The time of quiet contemplation and observation was past. Our animals kept us on our feet, at a trot, out of breath, and allowed us no more peaceful hours.

The Farm Animals

The farm animals poured in, in groups, in pairs, and one at a time. The original chickens were followed by fifty eight-week-old Rhode Island Reds. These are red-feathered chickens of a breed that serves two purposes: they lay good eggs, and at the same time have tender meat. They are therefore called edible layers.

Our original chickens belonged to another dual-purpose breed, the Barred Plymouth Rocks. This was a symbolic name for them, since they were our "rocks of strength" in the stormy, breaking waves of our chicken yard.

We ordered the Rhode Island Reds from a farm that sold pullorum-free chickens. These are chickens that are free of a kind of bacteria that is transmitted by the mother hen to the egg and makes the chickens sick in the second week of their lives and ripe for an early death. The disease, also called chicken dysentery or white diarrhea, is a major cause of loss in raising chickens and can only be controlled by selecting the mother hens.

To make this possible the USDA publishes a paper every year for the chicken-producing states that lists, with names and addresses, those chicken farms whose chickens have been checked and approved for the absence of the pullorum bacillus, just as they do for cattle that have been checked for tuberculosis or brucellosis.

Winnetou and I drove over to a farm that had been checked for pullorum to pick up our healthy chickens.

We had removed the rear seat of the car, covered the upholstery and the seat back with cloths, removed the carpets and laid newspapers on the floor.

By taking these precautions, we made our car keep some of the elegance that belongs to a two-tone Oldsmobile in spite of years of carrying chickens, goats, and pigs.

We wanted the chickens packed in chicken crates, but the farmer didn't have any available. So he stuffed the stormily protesting poultry into ten oat sacks.

I cannot describe the horror we felt when we saw the hopping, rolling sacks in our car, heard the piercing shrieks, and smelled the infernal stench that terrified birds give off.

The trip lasted half an hour. We didn't dare open the windows of the car because the day was cold and the young chickens had just come from warm houses.

After a quarter of an hour, the sacks became quiet and motionless.

"Feel them and see if they're dead," I said to Winnetou, and I stepped on the gas to get home more quickly.

Winnetou knelt on the seat and leaned over to poke the sacks.

"They're still warm," she said.

When we arrived home, we carried the sacks to the chicken houses.

The young hens went into the second chicken house. Only when they were full grown and approaching the time of egg-laying were the best behaved and fittest of them allowed to join the original hens in the first chicken house.

The twenty-five roosters were put into two "ranges," small coops that looked like scattered doghouses and were set in the chicken yard to serve as secure night quarters and as day shelters in bad weather.

As we unpacked the young hens, they squawked and raged, ran frantically back and forth, shrieked and behaved like silly children on a school trip.

But when we opened the sacks to let out the young roosters, we thought at first that we had released madmen and howling dervishes.

They ran around in circles, without goal or direction, as if they had been suddenly struck blind. When we finally succeeded in driving them to the long feeding troughs, they ranged themselves along the feed, transformed into a still shrieking but compact mass. They looked like the totalitarian crowds we saw pictured in the press releases listening to their leaders.

These young roosters were a great plague and filled me with a deep revulsion for all chickenkind. They often reminded me of a gang of neglected children, delinquents with criminal tendencies.

They enjoyed nothing more than attacking the weak among them, and they employed most effective methods for the systematic terrorization of their victims.

When they had been with us scarcely a month, they did such a shameful thing that I had no pity for them when it was their turn to be slaughtered. One day they picked out a weaker rooster and, in the truest sense of the words, drove him into a corner. They chased him until he ran his head into the stone wall of the chicken yard. Now, losing his reason completely, he hid his head in a deep, dark hole in the wall. What sport for our roosters to peck at the headless bird, stuck in the wall beating its wings, and to transform his body into a bloody pulp.

We heard the outcry, hurried out, and I drove in among the bloodthirsty roosters with the barn broom. They scattered as if the devil himself had come among them.

Zuck tried to release the head of the martyred rooster from the stone wall. He scarcely moved any more, and his body hung from his neck like a heavy sack on a string. There was nothing we could do but behead him. Later we freed his head from the wall with a crowbar.

How I hated my roosters!

The young hens were less wild and cruel, but they showed an unspeakable stupidity which filled me with a solid contempt for the animal kingdom.

Later, when we no longer bought young chickens, but let our own hens brood and the chicks hatch out of their eggs in our own yard, the picture changed substantially.

The silly, distracted, always anxious chickens developed into busy, thoughtful mothers. The new chicks, protected by these mothers, grew into young fowl who had learned from birth how chickens should behave.

The memory of the first weeks of their lives, when they were called to their feed by their mother's clucking, when the food was broken up into small bits for them by a motherly bill, and the times when the hens sheltered them under their wings from rain, cold, night, and danger, gave the new chickens a sense of security from chickhood on, something that the incubator chickens lacked.

The chicks that were raised in incubators behaved generally like a flock of restless orphans, always prepared for attack, always coming off badly, always defensive. With them we had to be prepared for anything.

I don't want to say anything against incubators. They are indispensable on large chicken farms, where they are set exclusively for mass production, and the good and bad instincts of the creatures can be regulated by mechanical devices to a certain extent.

Our farm, however, was small and not planned for mass production. Also, more than half of our animals appeared to have decided from the start to show off their individualistic tendencies and personal peculiarities without restraint — and to make us share their lives with them.

Often I had the impression that I lived in a colony of freakish personalities that demanded that we accept their special deviations and odd notions as the most natural and ordinary matters.

When the chickens were settled, we went to get the goats. Keeping goats is unusual in America. It is not that you are looked down on for keeping "the poor man's cow," but there is something mysterious involved in it. It seems almost as though you had come into a secret society of like-minded brothers and sisters, or had joined a religious sect. The articles about goats and goat products sound a little like the work of fanatic pamphleteers, and an atmosphere of faith-healing pervades them.

The simple facts are these: a goat needs one-fifth of the feed that a cow requires. It has enough room in a small stall. It is supposed to be easily satisfied (our goats were very demanding). A goat has only two teats instead of four, and is therefore faster to milk than a cow. The fat globules in goat's milk are smaller and cream development takes longer, so goat's milk is supposed to be more digestible than cow's milk. For this reason it is used for infants and for people with ulcers, whose stomach walls have been damaged by drinking too much fruit juice, or perhaps too much whiskey and gin. Babies and people with stomach trouble are the most profitable consumers of goat's milk. At a time when a liter of cow's milk cost twelve cents, you could sell goat's milk to hospitals for fifty cents a liter, or to private patients or infants for sixty-five cents a liter, so the milk of "the poor man's cow" brought in a very nice profit.

As for the much discussed flavor of goat's milk, goat milk enthusiasts claim that it has an aroma of almonds mixed with the bittersweet taste of fresh nutmeat skins, and its snow-white color indicates its precious purity.

The opponents of goat's milk say that it has a frightfully penetrating taste, and that the color makes them uncomfortable.

The people arguing for and against goat's milk seem to forget that taste can't be defined, is a product of what you are used to, and is closely connected to your individual imagination.

As for the disagreeable smell that goats and their milk sometimes have, no friend of goats denies it. But every intelligent goat owner knows that you must either not have a billy goat, or that he must pass his lonely life in seclusion, far from the ewes, since he is the carrier of the penetrating smell that gets into the stall, the coats of the ewes, the milk, the owner's clothing, the feed, and everything else it touches.

We had ordered two goats from a farmer in a small town about an hour away from our farm.

Waiting for us were an old pedigreed ewe, a Saanen with a long family tree — her grandfather's name was Prince Franz of Switzerland — and a quite young Saanen whose pedigree papers had been lost.

We had again removed the back seat of the car, hung the walls with white feed sacks, and covered the floor with layers of newspapers and sawdust, so that the car looked like a stall on wheels.

The goat owner was a pleasant man with a friendly family. His principal occupation was postmaster. On the side he raised goats, and on Sundays he played the trumpet in a band.

He led us to the meadow next to his house. There our future goats were tethered.

Even from a distance we could hear the ceaseless, low bleating of a goat. The owner explained that he would sell us the older Saanen at half price, in spite of her long pedigree, because she was a "bleater," and he had had run-ins with his neighbors on her account.

Our bleating Saanen had a mighty beard, no horns, and was named Heidi.

Heidi was snow white, looked very noble and wise, and simply couldn't stand solitude, as it very soon became evident. As long as she had human attention she stopped bleating, but scarcely was she left alone when she began to sound like a broken alpine horn. Since we had no neighbors, this damaged only our nerves, and they were long beyond repair.

The other Saanen, a little four-month-old kid, was tied to a stake with her sister. The little goats jumped about happily and full of life, but when one was loaded into our car the remaining one cried for her in such nameless despair that we felt like plantation owners cruelly separating a negro family at a slave market.

I exchanged a short glance of agreement with Winnetou, and soon we had bought the other little Saanen as well.

The reunion of the lively sisters was no small matter for our car.

But now Winnetou spent all the time, while I was busy loading the goats, discussing prices, and paying, with a small brown Toggenburg that lay wearily on the grass, studying us with sad eyes.

When Winnetou stroked her, she raised herself up on her short, weak legs and licked Winnetou's hand. The little goat's head was large, her coat long and rough, her body plump, and legs thin. She looked as if she had been put together wrong, and it was hard to guess her age.

"What's wrong with her?" Winnetou asked the owner. "And how old is she?"

"She is already a year old," he said, "but she is retarded. I tried out a new method of feeding on her, but it didn't suit her."

He wanted only eight dollars for the goat, and we now had another unintended goat in the car.

If our transportation of young chickens was disgusting, our transportation of goats was marked by an unbearable exhibi-

70

tion of tender affection.

I chauffeured, and Winnetou had the job of keeping the four goats off my neck.

The little Saanens put their forelegs on Winnetou's shoulders and nibbled at her hair. Heidi licked my neck and ears as though they were a block of salt. The goats' behavior and the tickling sent Winnetou and me into foolish, tortured giggles.

The Toggenburg rushed around among the other goats as if shut up in a too-small shipping cage, and she only stood still once in a while to let great lakes stream onto the sawdust and newspapers, inspiring the other goats to do the same.

By the time we reached the farm the car looked as though we had carried an entire kennel of dogs that were not yet housebroken, and with them a herd of deer that had left its droppings behind.

The car was such a mess that we decided to fetch the two pigs we had ordered the same day, so that we could combine the dirt and smell in one day, and not take it in installments.

It took several days of washing, scrubbing, and rinsing the car, and we had to dry it in the strongest sunlight before it got back its usual smell.

Zuck showed no surprise over the arrival of double the order of goats — by this time we could not be astonished, upset, or amazed by anything.

The Toggenburg reminded Zuck of a shaggy old dog we had once, and he named her "Mucki" after that ugly, bowlegged canine.

Mucki was put with Heidi in one section of the stall. The sisters, whom we called Flicki and Flocki, went into the other.

One outer wall of their roomy stall was made of movable slats that we could shove aside and thus let each goat stick her head through a separate hole to get at her dish of food. The food dishes were attached to a wooden bench in front of the openings and looked like a row of children's potties. The movable slats closed like horse collars around the goats' necks so that they had to eat their feed in peace and without mischief.

Once in the summer, when we brought our goats into a large shed that didn't have this carefully prepared arrangement for feeding them, their eating became an orgy of mischief. They threw the full dishes of food into the air and caught them on their noses. They turned water buckets into helmets. They fought over one dish, forgetting the three other dishes set out for them. In brief, the playfulness of goats knows no bounds, and their desire to play is beyond reckoning.

At first only Heidi needed to be milked, but in the course of time, when they had all become milk goats, Zuck began to train them.

It was a pretty sight and fun to watch when Zuck called their names, and one after the other they jumped eagerly and gracefully up onto the milking stand to be milked. The stand was made of a board a yard wide that during the day was fastened up to the wall with a hook, like a prison bed. At milking time we let the board down until it came to rest on a two-foot-high folding leg.

To milk we sat on a side extension of the platform, planned as a sort of stool for the milker.

This raised arrangement, this podium, is useful and convenient. Otherwise you have to sit or kneel on the floor to milk, since goats are only half as tall as cows.

You must be born a milker, or you have to have a feel for it. Zuck and Winnetou were outstanding milkers. I, however, did not seem to be born to milk, and had only the feeling that I hurt my hands, arms, and back by it. I groaned at the effort, took three times as long as was necessary, and on top of this I could not help suspecting that the goats were laughing at me.

The goats became the object of our heartfelt love and the reason for our wildest outbreaks of rage. They were fun and trouble, joy and vexation. They subjected our feelings to rapid swings between a desire to murder them and a wish to hug them tenderly.

The unruliest animal was Mucki.

When she was put on a normal diet and fed extra tidbits, sheared by Winnetou and so robbed of her shaggy coat, she grew large, strong, and long-legged.

She looked like a doe in the woods, so we locked her up when hunting season came and hunters invaded the woods. With the exception of the ball-playing sea lions and seals, goats are probably the animals that have the most fully developed sense of fun.

To state that goats eat everything, including tin cans, is just as mistaken as to say that a well-fed dog would rather take his meals from the garbage can.

For a dog a rotting bone is a delicacy that belongs to the same type of taste as Limburger or Camembert cheese, or highly flavored venison.

Goats are extremely fastidious creatures. They will eat no hay on which they have stood or lain, and no food that is not served to them in the cleanest manner.

Their unquenchable taste for roses, shoes, green apples, lawn chairs, pieces of laundry, and cigarette butts must come from the same impulse that leads well-fed small children to consume shoe polish like butter, to munch on matches like French fries, and to suck on candles like candy sticks.

Our four goats had 193 acres of land at their disposal, meadows, woods, streams, pastures, and rocks. In the morning they rushed off ready for any adventure, but after scarcely an hour they were back, trying to break into the vegetable and flower gardens, pulling laundry off the line, eating up the chicken feed, running into the living room and trying to make themselves comfortable in the armchairs by the fireplace. In short, they were everywhere that they didn't belong, and repeatedly brought all of our prevention schemes to nothing. We built fences against them around each garden, around trees, around the chicken houses. Soon we had ourselves ringed about as though we were in a palisade fortified against Indian attacks, but they still found ways to slip through.

There was nothing left to do but to go with them to the meadow, where at most they ate a couple of pages out of the books we brought along. Or we could stake them out. In spite of providing them with extra long chains and changing the position of the stakes several times a day, so that they always had new, fresh grass to eat, they complained and bleated in a way that broke our hearts. We let them loose again to make trouble.

On the same day that the goats arrived we brought home two pigs.

They were small, rosy animals, clean and happy. They were surely the most useful of our farm animals, but it was no fun to feed something alive three times a day only to be able, after a given time, to hang them up as hams, to pack them into barrels, and to preserve them in the freezer.

In addition to our planned purchases, we received an unexpected gift.

The owner of our general store drove up to our pond early one morning in his delivery truck and stopped there.

He handed over four ducks to us, two lovely brown and white ducks like wild ducks, and two fat white Peking ducks with yellow bills.

One of the white ducks, a drake, died of fatty degeneration of the heart shortly after his arrival.

The four ducks had lived until now on the village pond, where they had roused summer visitors out of their morning slumbers by immoderate quacking. The store owner was looking for a good home for the ducks where they couldn't wake or disturb anyone — except us.

He put them on the water, and they swam away as if it were their old familiar home. Then, quacking approval, they took possession of our pond.

We had published a notice in a farm newspaper that we were looking for geese. One Sunday afternoon an old Ford rattled up the hill.

On the front seat sat an old couple, while out of the back seat twisted the necks of two geese. Their bodies were tied up in brown feed sacks that we could hardly see in the clutter of tools, sacks, and gas cans.

When the old people took the geese out of the car and unwrapped them, the gander hissed at us threateningly and beat with his mighty wings like an angry swan.

The white goose that belonged to him was big, fat, and phlegmatic. The expression of her eyes and the way she held her head was so human in its stupidity that she reminded me immediately of a certain type of housewife and aunt. The term "silly goose" was clearly demonstrated in her.

We received an extra creature with the pair of geese. The farmer's wife released from another sack a small, dainty white duck with a yellow bill. It had hardly crept out of the sack when it collapsed on the grass half dead with fright.

At that moment the white gander plunged at the little duck as if he wanted to peck it to bits. But when he reached her, he stopped and touched her gently with his bill.

The little duck opened her eyes, got up, shook her feathers, and ran around behind the big gander as if she had never been upset. The big gander and the little duck went off to the pond, while the white goose stood there and looked after them with glassy blue eyes.

"They can't be separated," said the old farmer's wife, pointing to the departing pair, "the gander and the duck. He raised her. I won't charge anything for the duck," she added.

The farm couple climbed into their Ford and drove down the mountain. Little did they know what lessons in psychology they had arranged for us, and what unsolvable problems they had left behind.

Three geese and a drake were the concluding purchases of farm animals. The geese were magnificent specimens of the gray Toulouse breed. They cost five dollars apiece and were shipped to us by freight from Cape Cod.

The drake was a blue-green, black, and white bird of fabulous beauty. We bought him for the pond ducks which had been given to us, and we promised ourselves ducklings of heavenly beauty from the mating.

Now we were all set: the stalls were finished, the feed ready, the animals gathered around us, and we were about to take care of them according to all the rules of the art, systematically, properly, and expertly.

The practical skills were easily learned, but the imponderables and accidents were incomprehensible and innumerable.

We had begun the farm experiment with the illusion that it would be a foundation for our self-sufficiency and would give Zuck the possibility of doing his work.

He had had the choice of rowing as a slave in the Hollywood galleys with the convict's wages for forced labor or, on the other hand, doing his own work as his own master. But in America everything is always different and unforeseeable.

It is a riddle to me to this day how he found the time to write a play, to plan novels and stories, and sometimes even to compose a poem. As soon as he sat down in his room, we could be sure that the pigpen door would fall off its hinges, that a drake would become involved in a life-threatening fight with a gander, that the fireplace fire would start to smolder and drive clouds of smoke into his room, or that water from a cloudburst would pour through the roof into the kitchen.

He usually met these disturbances with a collection of German and American curses that brought approving grins even to the faces of the backwoods lumberjacks that often worked around our house.

But he always jumped up and did the job, because his other and true work had become rather abstract and uncertain at this point in his life. He had lost his voice and resonance, and he could at best carry on monologues with his desk drawer. Into this vanished the piles of outlines and sketches.

There we sat in our Noah's ark, shaken by storms and tempests, visited by torments, pursued by a chain of small disasters. We learned from them how to meet large catastrophes, how to deal with annoyances, and how to meet storms and tempests.

Confusion in the Chicken Yard

Soon we had a shed built between the two chicken houses. It connected them and was to serve as a shelter for the geese and ducks.

The white Muscovy ducks increased at an unexpected rate. Gussy, the asocial one, came home in the second summer with thirteen ducklings. Emma had twelve. Daughters of Gussy and Emma hatched two ducklings each. In short, the place was overrun with ducklings.

The duck families were put into individual small houses, but for the fall and winter there had to be housing for the remaining ducks that were not sold and not killed.

The geese had produced only eight goslings. We saved one of these, and so had to house six geese for the winter.

Now we could have made one section for ducks and one for geese in the new shed, but that wouldn't work for our feathered family.

During the day it was still possible to keep them together. They had the run of a wide area of meadows, water, and woods. But even there they formed distinct groups, while in the evening they collected into exclusive units opposed to each other.

To try to change these units was to risk death and destruction.

There were the six founding hens with their leader, the hen Elise, who formed the "gray family." They weren't exactly tyrannical, just domineering. They had taken over the leadership deliberately and peacefully — they tolerated only deliberate and peaceful chickens of other colors among them and threw nervous, squawking chickens out of their house without ado.

Here we should also note that nervous, anxious chickens are poor layers, and that you can tell good layers by their comb, eyes, legs, and behavior.

Therefore we picked out the most peaceful and best among the red chickens, the ones that the gray family couldn't object to, and put them in the gray house. Together with them it now had ten red and seven gray hens.

In the red house we had eighteen red leghorns. We thought that two roosters would be right for two chicken houses, but that was wrong, because one rooster was quickly killed off by the other.

These were two red roosters that we had picked out of the group of young roosters and had raised — probably brothers. In the first round of their fight, they were well matched. In the second round, one scratched out the eye of the other and so made him the weaker. In the third round, the stronger one dislocated the hip joint of the weaker. In the fourth, he bit his comb to pieces. In the last round, he scratched out the second eye and so made him totally blind. This cockfight went on during an entire week. We interfered as often as we could, but finally we had to kill the defeated rooster.

After his final conquest, the victor strutted about, bloodstained and proud, approached one or another hen absentmindedly, and then forgot his victory and went searching for worms.

That rooster belonged to the sort that are not concerned with reproduction, but with hunting for insects, larvae, and worms. He used to call the hens with a cry that was not much different from that of a mother hen calling her chicks, and then he divided his booty with his harem without assuring a proper share to himself. Sometimes he was so eager in his sharing that he began visibly to waste away, and we had to feed him an extra ration morning and evening to keep up his strength.

That rooster would now have remained the sole and uncontested ruler, if it had not been for the fighting cock Napoleon.

You see, we had a family of Bantam chickens that we had

78

bought because of their beauty and appeal.

They were silver "Sabright Bantams" belonging to the category "ornamental" fowl. Their black-bordered silver feathers, dark beaks, and slate-blue legs made them the real decoration of the chicken yard.

They are not as heavy as domestic chickens, can really fly, and choose the highest beams in the chicken house for sleeping.

Their little eggs taste something like pewit eggs when hard-boiled, and since the family multiplied, we had to kill and eat some of the chickens from time to time and therefore knew that the meat tasted like a cross between pigeon and partridge.

At first we acquired only a pair, and since the feathers of the Bantam hen reminded me of the coronation cloak of Josephine Beauharnais, we called her Josephine and her rooster Napoleon.

Now one of the characteristics of these wild fowl is that many of the roosters are quite belligerent.

So it happened not infrequently that our Napoleon, small and light, weighing hardly a pound and a half, shot down from the chicken house roof, plunged onto the head of the large chicken yard rooster, and was so nimble in his attack that the giant had to give way before the dwarf.

But when Napoleon forgot his small size and dared to attack from the ground, the fight was dangerous for him, and he was saved from certain death only by our timely intervention.

Sometimes Napoleon even attacked us.

He began by dragging his right wing like a toreador's cloak on the ground, coming ever closer in rapid circles, and suddenly, breaking out of the last circle, lunging at us and pecking at our knuckles with his sharp beak.

When he was angry I didn't dare approach him unless armed with a broom.

In the first year we had them, Napoleon and Josephine produced a little chicken that we named Lisettchen.

She stayed constantly with her parents and became a special creature. Sometimes when I went through the chicken houses in the evening to see that everything was in order, Lisettchen would flutter down from her sleeping perch on a rafter, sit on my shoulder or on the edge of a feed bucket, and wait for the tidbit I had for her.

79

When she had received her piece of stale white bread, two or three shreds of raw meat, or some coarsely ground corn, she would fly, with her bill still full, back to her parents. Annoyed at being disturbed, they took the rest of her treat out of her bill and pecked at her a little.

Below the Bantams' rafters was the pen of the white Muscovy ducks, those shy, mute birds who can't quack or gabble and only rarely make a noise that sounds something like the sounds made by a deaf mute.

Among the Muscovies there were three with names: besides Gussy and Emma there was the drake Emil, who had grown as big as a goose. Emil was quarrelsome, strong, and pugnacious and was glad to take on the ganders.

It was good for him that our wolfhound kept track of the poultry yard and not only drove away foxes, skunks, martens, and weasels, but also plunged bravely in between fighting animals and separated the combatants, not without pulling out a few of their tail feathers.

This intervention in their battles was the more important because the others were with reason afraid of the white gander, who often came flying at them, pursued them, and bit them vigorously in the tail feathers.

This white gander was probably the most difficult creature we had in the poultry yard.

He was large, strong, crafty, hot-tempered, and he gazed maliciously out of his bright blue eyes.

We called him Hermann, and the white goose that came with him Thusnelda. Both were Emdens, while the other geese were all gray Toulouse geese.

The little white duck that Hermann brought with him we called Herminchen.

Herminchen joined the three lake ducks we had been given. The big fat one was a Peking like Herminchen, and the other two were pretty brown and white Indian river ducks.

We named the river ducks Solvejg and Eleonora. We couldn't find a name for the fat one and didn't really want to because she promised to be a tender roast.

We named our animals, not by whim and fancy, but rather because the animals themselves forced us to give them certain names by their appearance, behavior, or some turn of fate.

Whoever had a name, however, could no longer be sold, butchered, or eaten and had the chance of dying a natural death.

The named ones seemed to understand this privilege with time. We could see their growing trust, which led on the one hand to an unusual tameness and affection, or on the other to a solid, dependable hatred, like that which the duck Gussy or the gander Hermann had for us.

The nameless ones, in contrast, never gave up entirely their fidgety, anxious behavior, since they probably sensed that their lives would end sooner or later under the knife.

The fat duck with the yellow beak escaped this fate because she acquired a name in time, even though it was not from us.

It happened this way: one Sunday some farm folks we didn't know came by our pond. They stopped their auto, and the woman stepped out and stood on the bank.

I was not far from the pond and watched the strangers and wondered what they wanted. Now the woman went quite close to the water, put her hands up to her mouth like a megaphone, and called with a loud voice: "Ssu-sie, Ssu-sie." Then our fat little duck separated herself from the flock of swimming geese and ducks and made her way over to the bank, constantly nodding her head. She waddled up to the woman and stopped in front of her. The woman had meanwhile noticed me and motioned me to come to her. "That is Susie," the woman said to me. "Look, she still knows me." She pointed to the duck, who was waddling around her, quacking and quacking.

"That was my Susie," the woman continued. "I brought her up. She was the most obstinate animal on the whole farm — that's why she became my favorite. Isn't she stubborn?" she asked me, beaming. I nodded my agreement vigorously and with conviction.

"Later we gave up keeping ducks, and I had to send her to the lake," she said, "and I have been looking for her a long time since she was missing from there. And today I said, 'Bill, we want to go and see if Susie has found a good place.' " I urged "Bill" to get out of the truck and to come with his wife to see the shed where her Susie lived.

"A good shed, a big pond," said the farmer's wife approvingly, and then they said goodbye.

When they had left, Zuck and Winnetou appeared and asked who the strangers were.

"Susie's parents," I explained and pointed to the fat duck with the air of making an introduction, "and this is Susie."

Susie was evidently pleased to be called by name, but that didn't make her at all more eager for company or less stubborn.

Susie, Eleonora, Solvejg, and Hermine lived together day and night, and with them lived Hermann, the gander.

Hermine had brought him into this circle of ducks, and what happened after that no one could really explain.

The four ducks would not be separated from Hermann. They waddled in front or in back of him, or they stood around him in an admiring circle.

For his part, Hermann had developed such a deep and obvious passion for the four that he left the herd of geese and the white goose Thusnelda and lived with the four ducks in bondage and depravity.

Of course we stopped him from spending the night with them as well, but it took real circus tricks to separate him from the ducks in the evening.

Every evening between five and seven o'clock, depending on the time of year, we heard an excited quacking and gabbling from the direction of the shed, mixed with the trumpeting of the gander. Immediately two of us had to stop whatever we were doing and run to the shed, for if we ignored this homecoming call, the four ducks and their Hermann would turn right around and disappear to spend the night in the open and make us worry for fear a fox would carry them off.

So there stood the four ducks and Hermann in front of the shed, clamoring for admittance.

Now we divided the work this way: One of us had to open the door, drive the ducks quickly into their pen, and slam the door shut again in front of Hermann's beak.

Hermann had to be held in check until the ducks had been locked in their pen. Then the door was opened a second time, and Hermann was driven out of his arena into his cage like an angry tiger. Where the passageway led past the duck pen, Hermann behaved like a madman, and it was hard work to force him to go into the goose pen. Without the broom we could not have controlled Hermann, who was wild and dangerous. In fact, the broom often played an important role in driving the animals home, in separating fighters, and in self-defense.

They were all afraid of the broom: the fowl, the dogs, the cats, all the animals except the goats, who even went so far as to nibble at the broom straw.

It was not that we beat the animals with the broom, or even touched them.

We just had to hold the broom in front of us, like a witch who is ready to mount her broomstick to ride to the Blocksberg, and the animals scattered and took to flight in the desired direction.

Even the hair on the cats began to stand on end, and they arched their backs and started to spit when the stubbly face of the broom approached them. It seemed almost like a magical fear of the witchly attributes that made the animals run away.

It was not only important to bring the animals into the safety of the sheds at night, but the biggest part of the task was to arrange them according to their natural order and to direct their unnatural inclinations in natural paths. That is, we aimed to put the ganders with the geese, the drakes with the ducks, and to erase at night the line they drew through our calculations by day. For this purpose a beautiful Canadian drake, Goesta, was put with the ducks. Now you might assume that it would be an easy job to bring Goesta into the pen with the four ducks. Goesta had been interested from the first day in the white Muscovies and had gotten into a serious battle with the Muscovy drake Emil about it several times. But the handsome Goesta found no favor with the four ducks—every evening they greeted him with shrill insults that sounded like the scolding of old maids.

Goesta would first look at the four with evident disgust. Then he would drive them away from the feed trough to have the feed for himself. When he was full he swung himself up onto his sleeping perch and paid no attention to the angry ducks, who only quieted down when they heard the loud, longing cry of Hermann from the goose pen.

In the goose pen was a gray gander, who got along amazingly well with Hermann, probably because he had noticed that Hermann wasn't interested in the geese. Then there were still three gray geese and the abandoned Thusnelda. Thusnelda was absolutely true to Hermann, and when she was once attacked by a young gray gander in an unmistakable way, she knocked out one eye of her unhappy suitor.

These emotional complications and confusions, these tangled relationships among the animals, struck many uninvolved observers as most puzzling and amusing. In the first year we didn't even suspect ourselves the extent of the consequences.

It was just our luck that Thusnelda was the best and most dependable brood goose, and Solvejg as well as Eleonora turned out to be the most attentive mothers.

When their time came, they built themselves nests, laid their eggs in them, and began at the proper interval to brood devotedly.

When this happened the first time, we could not imagine that the spinsterish ducks and the scorned Thusnelda were sitting on nothing but infertile eggs out of which no young thing would come.

Eleonora showed us what that meant.

Eleonora settled herself on ten eggs and brooded. She brooded with truly fanatic devotion, and we had trouble driving her off every evening to take a little break, eat her food in peace, wash herself in the water bowl, and afterwards move about a little. Usually she gulped down quickly a bit of the feed we had specially prepared for her, ran to the water bowl and sprinkled her belly feathers, filled her beak with water after a few hasty sips, ran back to the nest and carefully sprinkled the eggs one by one after turning them tenderly with her beak. This sprinkling softens the shells and makes it easier for the ducklings to break through when they hatch. Eleonora was a duck mother who took care of everything, from proper treatment of the egg shells to even distribution of brooding warmth. For this purpose she had upholstered her nest with the finest breast feathers.

There she sat for twenty-eight days and waited for the tapping and knocking in her eggs.

We waited with her, but nothing stirred or moved and everything remained still as death in her nest.

Eleonora began to grow visibly thinner and to decline. We let her sit five days more, but when we came into the shed on the thirty-third brooding day, we were met by a terrible stench.

We found Eleonora the picture of total insanity, rolling her eggs out of the nest and tearing it to pieces. The half-open eggs showed no trace of a young duck, or even of an embryo. They were filled with a greenish yolk-like liquid, whose pestilential smell was far worse than rotten eggs.

We picked up Eleonora and held her fast, although she struggled wildly to return to her dirty nest, and we washed her breast and belly feathers, which were stuck together with the green putrefaction from the broken eggs. We carried her to the pond to finish her purifying bath.

For several days she tried day and night to return to her nest, but we had removed and burnt it, cleaned up everything, and locked the door tightly.

In spite of the danger from predatory animals, we left her on the pond for three nights to keep her away from the empty nest and the company of the others.

Several times in the night we heard her quacking piteously in front of the shed door, asking to get in, and the others answering from inside.

Then she went back again, swam in great circles around the dead trees that rose out of the pond, and as she dove into the cool water, washed her feathers, and began to beat her wings with new strength, she seemed to separate herself farther and farther from her despair and the deep madness that had overcome her.

After this disaster we learned what we must do, and we set out to correct nature.

First we acquired a candling apparatus, and as the brooding time approached again we gathered the eggs of all the ducks and geese and left them for a week in the cellar.

Meanwhile I wrote to the different farms that had advertised in our farm paper: "Hatching eggs from Toulouse, Emden, Chinese and African geese, and Muscovy, Rouen, and Indian river ducks."

Usually we received the answer: "Dear friends, unfortunately I am unable to send you hatching eggs since all my geese and ducks are already sitting, but I can send you some when they are hatched. . ."

Sometimes there were eggs.

After eight days we brought the eggs that our fowl had laid out of the cellar, darkened the kitchen, and tested them one after the other on the candling apparatus. This was a square tin box with an electric bulb in it. On the upper side of the box a hole had been cut and lined with rubber. We set the eggs on this and turned on the light and could look into every part of the lighted egg to search for the dark spot that meant that the egg had been fertilized.

The unfertilized eggs were used for cooking. We took the eggs for hatching back to the sheds.

The guaranteed eggs we put in the nests of Thusnelda, Eleonora, and Solvejg, exchanging them secretly with the empty, unproductive eggs they had laid.

The chickens were no problem.

We had little brooding houses for them, one for each hen mother. They came already assembled from Sears and Roebuck and looked like tiny doghouses.

Usually the brooding hens needed only a day to get used to their new quarters and caused little trouble.

The geese had two big brooding houses near the pond and usually used them for this purpose. The ducks, on the other hand, couldn't decide whether they wanted to be domesticated or wild birds and nested under stone walls, in the cellars of old barns, in rain barrels, and in holes in the ground, and we had a great deal of trouble finding them and moving them carefully with their nests into the security of the duck shed.

Such moving never succeeded with Gussy, because we could never find her. Some of the other Muscovy ducks we had to leave where they were because by the time we found them it was too late for moving. Then we watched anxiously for the appearance of the ducklings, which we had to protect immediately against fox and weasel.

Once one of the Muscovy duck mothers succeeded in hiding her new family from us. She led them immediately after birth out of a hole in the ground to the pond. There six of the eleven perished, and we were only just able to rescue the rest from the water in time.

The difficulty with domestic animals is that, no matter how wild they act, they have lost a large part of the instinct that they doubtless had when they were still untamed wild animals.

They let themselves be tamed, trading their freedom for housing and care, an apparent but temporary security, and left it to their caretakers to watch over their life, their health, and their activities.

We had to take care day and night that they did not eat too much, wrong or even poisonous things, and that they didn't drive their young into the water too early. We had to deal with their various illnesses, with which they could not cope themselves. In short, watching over and caring for the animals consisted primarily in protecting them from their own mistakes and putting a timely barrier in the way of their dangerous inclinations.

Among our errant ones was even Thusnelda, to whom it occurred about the end of April, when it was still very cold and there was much snow on the ground, to build her nest under the little corncrib that stood on six legs and was used to dry the corn.

The fowl, who were let out of the sheds summer and winter, had often gone under this corncrib, so that we paid no particular notice and only discovered Thusnelda's completed nest too late.

Since she was a particularly difficult "case," we didn't dare move her, but had to build a whole shed around her to protect her from cold and snow, and we set up a watch to keep foxes, skunks, and weasels away from her.

In the evening we had the dogs run around the corncrib and sniff through everything looking for small predators, so that the air and ground around the goose Thusnelda was filled with the wolf smell of the dogs. We expected that this frightening fragrance would give Thusnelda some protection.

My bedroom was right across from the corncrib, and in that brooding month I ran down to the barn in the middle of the night innumerable times because I thought that I had heard a noise.

Then I lit up every corner with the flashlight, last of all the nest itself where Thusnelda was sitting on her eggs, which came from Harwich, Massachusetts. She looked at me angrily with her stupid blue eyes, as if I had disturbed her rest, not she mine.

When her goslings hatched, four yellow-green, strong,

incredibly small geese, Hermann suddenly and unexpectedly turned up, rushed at the goslings, and before I could get a broom he was close to the nest.

I was sure that there would now be a battle with Thusnelda, and in it all the newborn geese would be trampled and pecked to death. I stood there with that helpless feeling of despair with which you watch the hail fall from heaven and destroy the harvest.

Then something entirely unexpected happened.

Thusnelda did not defend herself, nor did she try to defend her babies or to take them under her wings. The four little puff balls on their too-long legs chirped at the big bird, and Hermann laid his head to one side and looked at them with that heavenly blue glance that he usually saved for Herminchen. The whole thing was a misunderstanding.

It was a misunderstanding first of all on my part, since I had believed that Hermann would act like most ganders, drakes, and even roosters who sometimes show murderous intent toward young animals, even when they are their own sons and daughters.

On the other hand Hermann also had a misunderstanding. Unpredictable as he was, he went from one extreme to the other and without transition became a devoted family man, even though he was not at all the father of these geese who came from Massachusetts.

From that hour on, he left the four ducks and walked in front of his assumed family, ready to defend them against every attack. Thusnelda waddled after them, and the procession of the six geese reminded us of a bourgeois family in modest circumstances on a Sunday outing where the father had decided to treat the family to something.

While Hermann had, so to speak, goosestepped from one unnatural situation to another, his ducks had meanwhile been sitting on the strange eggs which had been slipped into their nests and had become very busy and good mothers.

When the young ducks had their feathers and no longer needed their mothers, they went back together and all became just as prudish, peculiar, and whimsical as before, so that no one would ever think that these spinsterish creatures had ever spent even a day hatching eggs.

In early fall the young geese had also become large, strong birds, who no longer needed the protection and guidance of a father.

Then Hermann left them and Thusnelda as suddenly as he had come and went back to his ducks.

This sequence of events repeated itself every year in the same way.

It seemed as if the four ducks and the gander took a couple of weeks a year from their unusual common life to make an excursion into the natural life.

In these vacation times, their outstanding capacities as mothers and fathers became so apparent that, just on that account, we couldn't get rid of them. They were not willing to make even the smallest change in their way of life, their character, or in their confusing activities. As soon as it was fall, they went back together and forgot completely that in spring and summer they had been useful farm animals, indulging again their unfruitful inclinations.

Nevertheless, with time a peaceful cooperation developed between them and us with happy results. When spring came, we soon forgave whatever annoyance and trouble they had given us by their absurd behavior.

So they and we drew certain boundary lines, behind which they could forget the natural and we the unnatural, they in the fall and we in the spring.

The Rats

It was the third summer.

That was when I saw them for the first time.

It was evening, and I had gone into the shed to mix the feed before dark.

In this shed the buckets in which the feed was kept stood across from the entrance in a long row.

There was laying meal, feed grain, and the mash for fattening the chickens. There were buckets for duck and goose feed, which we mixed ourselves.

Zuck had carried the heavy sacks into the shed for me and left them in front of the empty buckets.

I began to untie the strings of the sacks and to use a measuring scoop to fill the buckets with the prescribed amounts of oats, bran, fattening mash, and corn meal.

The quiet of evening filled the shed. Ducks and geese peeped in their sleep. Lisettchen sat above me on her beam. I called her name, but this evening she only blinked at me and wouldn't fly down.

The feed rattled into the buckets and smelled like fields at harvest time.

Suddenly I stopped in the middle of my work, because a violent, overwhelming terror seized me, like the fear of the unaccustomed and unknown. I felt suddenly that I was not alone with my animals, that I was being watched closely from some corner.

I stood motionless and waited.

Now I heard a noise—a disembodied, ghostly tripping across the wooden floor. Then I saw something standing on the stairs. It was a large, gray-brown rat.

I still didn't move and stood face-to-face with the rat, who watched me with quiet menace.

Then I did something stupid. Instead of throwing a metal lid, a shovel, or a knife at it, I clapped my hands like a magician who wants to make something appear or disappear, and the rat escaped, whole and unhurt.

I ran into the house, where Zuck and the children sat around the supper table, waiting for me.

"What took you so long?" they asked me.

"Something terrible has happened," I said. "We have rats."

We ate supper about midnight.

We took the dogs out of the kennel and brought them to the shed. They howled and whined and finally found the entrances to the tunnels the rats had dug under the chicken houses and the shed.

Then we went into the shed and the chicken houses and switched on the lights. This woke the birds, who broke out in bright morning crowing, cackling, quacking, and gabbling.

We knelt down among the frightened birds who had jumped down from their sleeping perches to demand food, and we crept into every corner with flashlights to look for rat holes.

In the red chicken house we found one among the nests and nailed it up with strong, fine-meshed hardware cloth. In the shed itself we could do little. There the rats had gnawed away whole boards under the stairways and thresholds that led to the chicken houses.

We nailed up the boards and plugged and screened the holes, but there were too many places they had broken through already to keep them out of the middle shed. The ducks and geese were in no danger when awake, and the rats would not attack the larger chickens, but all of the smaller birds and the young poultry had to be protected from them.

So I climbed up the ladder and took Lisettchen, Josephine, and Napoleon from their sleeping perch and brought them into the safe gray chicken house.

The damage the rats did in the first summer they were at our farm was frightful. Their first attack was like a blitzkrieg.

They took thirty-two ducklings, eight chicks, and three newborn geese.

Our enemies were not mere house rats, but an army of itinerant Norwegian rats. They march across the countryside in formation, and when a farm pleases them they call a halt, besiege and occupy it.

They build their dugouts quickly and secretly under the sheds and houses they intend to plunder. Almost before they have finished their living quarters, they begin to gnaw tunnels into the sheds at night to reach the feed, the eggs, and the young animals.

Some things are eaten on the spot, but most of the booty is taken away through the rat holes into their tunnels. The way they carry out their raids, the removal of the booty, their disappearance and reemergence in unexpected spots all left us no doubt that we were dealing with an uncannily well-organized and functioning rat state.

We were set under siege by them, and our actions during the first days were very much like the hasty digging of trenches.

Because we had to work quickly, and you cannot pour cement floors in haste, we built cages around the mothers and their endangered young, through whose grids not even the smallest and youngest rat could slip. The broodhouses which stood in the meadow were no longer safe from the rats, and we had to build cage after cage, so that our sheds and barns, all divided into cells, soon looked like Sing-Sing prison.

In this battle with the rats, Lisettchen, who had become a mother for the first time, was robbed of her four tiny Bantam chicks. Why the rats had spared the little Bantam hen herself can only be explained by the fact that Lisettchen broke out in such an enraged outcry and beat so wildly with her wings that even the rats must have been frightened off. We had put Lisettchen in a particularly strong wire cell, but the rats had eaten through the double wood floor.

Now, while Zuck and Winnetou plugged the rat hole and spread wire mesh over the entire floor of the cell, I tried to calm Lisettchen, who was lamenting so bitterly that we could hardly stand it. In my despair over her pain, I decided to try a daring experiment. There were still two Bantam mothers with five chicks each. I reached under their wings and took two young from each mother. Then I put the four Bantam chicks in Lisettchen's nest.

I don't believe that I could have deceived Lisettchen in this way under normal circumstances, but shock had blurred her ability to discriminate.

When I put her back on the nest, she looked for only a moment at the four new chicks, who were two weeks older than her own stolen chicks. Then she took the four strangers under her wings, still breathing heavily as though she had been roused from a frightening dream.

In our farm paper appeared the following item:

"Rats cost American farmers sixty-three million dollars a year. Their population is approximately the same as the human population of the United States. Half of the rats live on farms. The cost of one rat is about two dollars a year. See your nearest USDA office or consult your local Farm Bureau agent about ways to control these pests."

We estimated the rat population on our farm at fifty to sixty. The consumption allotted to them, at two dollars a year, had been eaten up in the first three months after their arrival.

Therefore we decided to escalate our attack to a war of extermination. Before I describe the phases of this war, I must first establish the fact that we were not afraid of rats.

When I saw the first one in the barn, it was not her appearance that filled me with paralyzing fear, but the realization that she was without doubt only an outpost of an army of rats lurking in the background. I merely experienced the shock of a tower guard who sees the first enemy appear on the horizon.

I could not be frightened or disgusted by the rats because their conscious intelligence and calculated menace made them an equally matched foe. They had neither the unknown, indefinable frightfulness of spiders, scorpions, and snakes, nor the dull repulsion of potato bugs and grubs, vermin that do not know why they do damage. I lived with the rats long enough to have the opportunity to look them in the eye often.

In those rat eyes I found a kind of consciousness, a knowledge of their undertakings and deeds that lifted them out of the level of vermin into that of a proper enemy.

It was once announced in a newspaper article that a scientist had finally found the bones of the orangutan from which we must all be descended. Tied to that discovery was the amazing theory that, after humankind, rats or ants would take over the dominion of the world. If I accepted the idea of this dark utopia for a moment, I'd bet on the rats.

We began the first phase of our war with an open attack which miscarried. For this failure neither the rats nor we were to blame, nor even the method we chose, but a thirteen-year-old boy we had hired to help, but who helped very little.

The method was simple.

You drove your car up to the building, took all the animals out, shut the windows and doors, and plugged the cracks carefully, as though you wanted to commit suicide with gas.

Then you fastened the garden hose to the exhaust of the car, brought it through a hole the size of the hose into the building and in front of a rat hole, turned on the motor, and sent the poisonous, death-bringing exhaust fumes into the rat tunnels and the building.

I was enthusiastic about this modern chemical method, and everything was prepared down to the smallest detail.

But in the last moment before I started the motor, my cautious, mistrustful Zuck made one more last round through the shed, climbed a ladder, and found our hired boy with my pet cat in his arms, buried in the hay, fast asleep with a cigarette butt in his mouth.

So we abandoned our life-threatening gassing method and turned to simple rat poison. Setting rat traps was dangerous to the young animals, and poisons containing arsenic were menacing to all, but a paste had been invented that was supposed to be harmful only to rats.

How and when this paste was to be used required psychological preparation. Now the second phase began, the part that we called the "phony war."

For ten days we put down clean bacon and cheese rinds in the sheds and chicken houses to make the rats feel secure.

It is noteworthy that the rats did not appear in the goat and pig barn. Also they almost never came into the cellar of our house. Because of that they were all the more firmly entrenched where the poultry lived.

I had reached a kind of agreement with the rats. When I

entered the middle shed where the feed buckets stood, I clapped my hands. At this signal the rats disappeared into their holes. Once a rat in its haste jumped from the hayloft onto my shoulder, using it as a springboard to the floor.

That was not a pleasant sensation!

On each of the ten evenings when I distributed bacon and cheese, the rats came back out of their nooks and crannies and crouched behind the feed buckets. I acted as though I were preparing tidbits for the poultry, who are known to eat scraps, meat, and fat with relish.

The chicken coops on their stone foundations were relatively safe from the rats. Even there, though, the possibility existed that they would use the flap doors that were planned for the daily entrance and exit of the chickens and hide themselves inside in the evening.

Zuck found just such a stowaway rat in the gray chicken house one evening on his final tour of inspection.

He had a shovel in his hand and forced the rat into a corner with it.

It was a fully grown, large rat. When Zuck prepared to strike, it turned like lightning and jumped to the attack.

Now on the same day Zuck had cleaned out the pigpen, and luckily was still wearing high boots. These protected him from the rat's sharp, dangerous bite. Zuck succeeded in killing the rat, but we all felt rather ill the entire evening and could not stop telling grisly stories we had heard and read. The talk came around again and again to the almost unconquerable cunning and devilishness of rats, and to their love of attacking their attackers.

We talked about fingers that had been bitten off and festering leg wounds that people battling rats had sustained. We often glanced furtively and with shuddering at the high boots that stood in the corner of the kitchen and showed the marks of the rat's teeth at knee height.

On the following day the battle began in earnest.

Zuck and I shut ourselves in the workshop, taking care that no animal could get in, and mixed our poison.

We put on rubber gloves which we had earlier rubbed on the coats of our goats so that no human smell would betray us or show that our fingers were involved in the game. We had

96

brown pans with green paste in them, and we rubbed the paste carefully into the pieces of bacon and the cheese rinds.

The green paste contained a poison that had the effect of making the rats thirsty and driving them to water. After drinking the water in the open, far from their hiding places, they died.

That is, it was a type of poison that discouraged the rotting of the dead rats in their holes and so prevented the pollution of the air and the development of unhealthy germs.

On the evening of the eleventh day we brought the poisoned bacon and cheese bits over to the shed.

I clapped my hands as always, whereupon the scratching and tripping of claws began, as in a haunted house that has been abandoned by men and taken over by rats. Now Zuck checked that all the animals were locked in their Sing-Sing cells.

Then we pulled on our rubber gloves and distributed the poisoned morsels.

While doing this we spoke casually and loudly about ordinary things to give the impression that, in spite of the gloves, we were doing everyday, ordinary things. But I couldn't get rid of the feeling that one of the oldest rats, one that I thought I knew and considered a member of the highest rat council, was observing our actions closely and spitefully.

The next morning we were in the shed very early.

We had decided not to let a single animal out of the sheds, nor a dog out of the kennel, nor a cat out of the house for the entire day, so that they would not be poisoned by the dead rats.

When we came to the watering troughs for the poultry, which stood filled with water in the meadows, we found twenty dead rats in and around the troughs.

After we recovered from this ugly sight and started to remove the corpses, we noticed something horrible.

We went to the shed, opened the door quietly, and stood there without moving.

In the shed were twenty or thirty large, fully grown rats, who stared at us from all the corners. Only three of them took the trouble to disappear once more behind the feed buckets.

Outside, however, lay the corpses of small, half-grown rats, and there was not a single large, old rat among them.

We now knew that the experienced elders had sent their children ahead of them to see if there was death hidden in the bacon and the cheese rinds.

They had sacrificed the unwary, inexperienced rats, and by doing that had preserved a select group of the most dangerous and experienced ones. We realized that it would take other weapons to beat them than the ones we had available.

But still we built fences, gratings, and cages until our fingers and hands bled from wire-pulling, hammering, and nailing.

The rats could get at our animals less and less, but they gnawed into every feed sack as it arrived, and we had to buy more and more metal bins to protect the feed from their greediness.

Two years after their arrival they suddenly disappeared. Whether it was that we had really fooled them a few times, and a few of their elders had themselves gotten the poisoned corn, or whether it was that we had put up too many fences even an eel couldn't wriggle through, or whether it was simply that they were seized with wanderlust and went in search of a better farm, we never knew.

They left in the fall.

Their departure happened as secretly and invisibly as their arrival. The holes and passages looked like an abandoned mining operation. We repaired the marks of their gnawing in the wood, and the sickly sweet stench which they had spread disappeared after the big fall cleaning.

The barns and chicken houses belonged once more to the domestic animals and to us, and at night it was as quiet in the shed as it is at the time when one o'clock strikes from the church tower and the ghosts fly away and vanish.

Bulletin 1652

One morning, when I went to see the young chickens in the chicken house, I found traces of blood.

That was four weeks after we had started the farm. The pens were sparkling new, and the chickens had settled in well.

At first I thought there had been a fight, but then I noticed that most of the chickens looked different, a little like school-children that have eaten something forbidden and now hang their heads.

I let the chickens out as I always did, but they didn't crowd to the door as usual. Some stayed back in the shed and cowered together in a corner as if they were freezing, even though it was a warm morning.

About noon a farmer came by, bringing us a particular variety of seed potatoes from his farm. I took him to look at the chickens.

"Do you perhaps know what is wrong with the chickens?" I asked him.

He looked at the chickens and then went into the chicken houses and studied the blood spots on the perches.

"That's bad," he said. "How many chickens do you have?"

"Fifty young chickens," I answered, "and seven hens."

"The hens won't get it," he said, "but you will probably lose twenty-five to thirty of the young ones, perhaps even more. You can count on that."

"What can we do then?" I asked, horrified.

"Not much," he answered and shrugged his shoulders, "but

you can of course ask at the agricultural office."

At three o'clock in the afternoon, two chickens were dead. At four o'clock I was in the agricultural office in the next town. There they explained to me that, according to my description, it must be a case of coccidiosis, the red dysentery, a parasite disease which affects flocks and results in a high percentage of loss. There were known measures of prevention, but no sure way of treating it. I should however try the big feed store in the next town. They had medicine there. Then they put into my hand Farmers' Bulletin No. 1652, which deals with poultry illnesses.

I drove thirteen miles farther to the next town, where I arrived just as the store was closing. When I said "coccidiosis" and asked for a sack of "Flush" and one of "Pellets" — they had just taught me these expressions at the agricultural office — they handed me three kinds of medicine with an illustrated paper from the laboratory that told how to use them. In this paper I found pictures of chickens who had just the same cowering head-hanging pose that I had discovered that morning in our chicken house.

They loaded the two bags in for me, and on the return trip I stopped once more at a sawmill to get some sacks of fresh sawdust.

At seven o'clock I was back home again.

I had gone about sixty miles to get medicines and materials for disinfection and had brought back as well a little hope of salvaging something from total loss.

We set right to work. We tacked the paper with the illustrated description of coccidiosis on the wall and did exactly what was pictured there. We dissolved tablets in gallons of drinking water. We mixed two kinds of medicine into the feed meal and grain. When we were done, we brought the medicine-laced feed and drinking water over into the sheds, turned on the light, and woke the sleeping birds. Some of them were cowering on the ground because they were too weak to get up onto the perches. We fed them by hand to be sure that they also took some medicine. The others jumped down from their perches and went to the feed trough, for there is no hour, day or night, when chickens can't eat.

The night feeding was not at all prescribed, but we didn't

want to let another night pass without doing something about this sickness.

Early the next morning we built a fence that on one hand would separate the sick chickens from the healthy ones and on the other enclose a new run for the sick ones, since the old run was infected by their manure. The manure contained the coccidiae in the form of egg cysts and could transmit it.

When the fences were finished, we drove the chickens into the open, closed the chicken houses, and began to carry out a thorough cleaning of the buildings.

Zuck carried buckets of boiling water over and took the infected sawdust away to a place where he burned it. We washed all feed containers with water containing disinfectants and wiped perches, manure drawers, walls, and floors with a creosote solution. By noon everything had been thoroughly cleaned, and we smelled from head to foot like hospital attendants in the cholera ward. The thought of eating turned our stomachs.

Every day for five days we cleaned the chicken houses, changed the sawdust, fed the chickens with medicines, cleaned and rinsed them out with "Flush" and strengthened them with "Pellets."

Each morning we entered the chicken house with palpitations, expecting to find dead chickens, but not a single one more died.

After this triumph I did not want to wait until an illness broke out to go after remedies. Instead I set up beforehand an apothecary that contained everything from medicines to disinfectants to udder salves and louse powders — whatever could be obtained.

For this purpose I studied the farm bulletins, agricultural magazines, and advertisements from the laboratories. After reading these things I felt like a medical student who is coming into the clinic semester, or like a mother, expecting her first child, who has read all the popular literature about the birth process and now is quite certain that the birth will be abnormal and the child will be born crippled.

So I was prepared for all illnesses, but to our surprise we were spared chicken cholera, plague, tuberculosis, diphtheria, leukemia, gout, smallpox, and rickets. There were still, however, a large choice of diseases left, and soon I set up a hospital with different divisions so that I could isolate the sick animals and take care of them without interruption.

We seldom lost animals, but when one died of an unknown cause we packed it up according to instructions and sent the corpse to our nearest veterinary institute.

After a short time an answer came that either reassured us or disturbed us and told us what measures we should immediately take.

So, for example, one letter said: "The investigation of the red hen that you sent us showed a tumor of the inner organs, something that can have different causes and poses no serious threat to the other chickens. However, if there are further losses, I suggest that you send us two or three samples, and I hope that we can then give you a conclusive diagnosis of the condition of your poultry. Respectfully, ———, the veterinary pathologist."

For two years we had no sample cases to send.

Michaela, the gray founding hen, got frozen toes in the winter because she sat in the snow too much, but I put her in a cage in the kitchen in spite of Zuck's protests and quickly healed her there.

Then Maria, also one of the gray founding hens, got swollen, scabby legs in the summer, and we determined with the help of Bulletin 1652 that she had mites. That meant disinfecting chicken houses again and painting the perches with a tobacco solution since the mites, also called chicken lice, like best to lodge there so that they can suck the blood of the chickens at night.

Maria, who was generally so bright and understanding, showed the greatest displeasure when we dipped her scaly legs in crude oil. She stamped so that our hair, cheeks, and noses were drenched in oil and we smelled like gas station attendants. Maria, who had been hardly able to walk, recovered very quickly after this petroleum experience. We rubbed her legs with Peru balm and fed her the best greens and extra crumbs, and she soon forgave us for the crude oil treatment.

But then we had something serious.

One of Gussy's daughters bent her webbed duck's foot backwards one day, and then the second one, so that she lay helpless and after a short time perished miserably.

We sent her as a sample to Montpelier to the veterinary institute and received the answer: "The organs of the duck sent show no abnormality. We would be interested to discover the cause; could you therefore send us as soon as possible one or two of your lame ducks?"

No, we couldn't and wouldn't, for the next two lame ducks were Susie and the gigantic drake Emil. When we saw the two large, heavy creatures coming home for the first time, limping and dragging a foot, we were filled with foreboding, for we saw ahead of us the painful end that the nameless sample-duck had suffered.

So I read all the parts of Bulletin 1652 that dealt with foot ailments and lameness. The symptoms were not clear, but closest to "bent-toe" was a disease that comes from vitamin deficiency.

Susie's and Emil's feet had toes that were more than bent. Emil's right and Susie's left foot looked as if they were broken and all the ligaments torn. They walked on the top surface of the dragged foot and scratched and tore the skin.

Winnetou, who was at this time playing with the idea of becoming a veterinarian, put the feet in splints to bring them into a normal position. Then we separated the ducks and put them on beds of straw to begin a diet rich in vitamins.

We fed them a mixture of wheat bran, barley, meat, charcoal, and salt, to which we added a good dose of vitamin B complex and liver extract. Then we mixed the whole to mush with goat's milk. Sometimes I even put yeast into the mixture and let it grow. Twice a day we fed them bowls full of clover, soybean leaves, pea leaves, and similar things. Every day we dipped the two ducks in the wash basin and dried them in the sun, and we forced them to take daily exercise limping on one leg.

Susie accepted this treatment sullenly, but Emil, the albatross, could hardly be held and beat us with his wings like a vulture.

The injuries that we got from taking care of the animals were too many to list here. It should just be noted that we kept in our animal dispensary large bottles of iodine and bandages for *our* injuries.

Since everything always happened at the same time on the farm, it was just at the time when Winnetou and I were busiest taking care of Susie and Emil that Flicki gave birth to two little goats, and Flocki had serious difficulties so that Zuck had to draw three little kids out of her with his hands. Meanwhile Heidi had no young, but picked up an udder infection. Milking became a problem, and the hospital was full.

Finally the day we anticipated and feared arrived, when we were to take the bandages off Susie's and Emil's feet.

They had both become gentle as lambs from the special treatment and unusual diet. Emil no longer struck us with his powerful wings, but lay in our arms and gazed about dreamily.

I cannot really describe that moment, neither the fear we had as we removed the bandages, nor the joy we felt when both ducks climbed out and waddled off to the pond on straight, unbent feet to begin a normal life again.

For a long time they acted like convalescents, appearing daily at the kitchen door and demanding extra handouts, which they always received.

Susie became mild and good natured toward us and quacked like a Walt Disney duck who wants to show that she is happy.

Emil became peaceful and wise after his illness and could be seen evenings sitting together with Goesta, the Canadian drake, on a rock by the pond. He seemed to have forgotten that he had ever hated this rival, and an elegaic and gentle evening mood lay over them both.

The sicknesses I have talked about were all regular, proper diseases that you could call by name. You could diagnose the symptoms, try to find the cause, and proceed to treatment and prevention.

It seems to me that too little attention is paid to the personal treatment of animals, although some work is beginning to be done on animal psychology. I am convinced that the enormous losses that farmers suffer every year through animal illnesses could be significantly reduced if the sick animals were shown somewhat more personal interest in addition to sulfa and penicillin, and that it would strengthen their immunity and take away their gloomy desire to die.

One day something new came up, something we were totally unprepared for — insanity.

Again we found flecks of blood in the chicken houses, but this time even walls, floors, and feeding troughs were spattered with blood, and we could see that the chickens were not just scrapping as usual, but had begun to peck at each other in earnest and to inflict dangerous wounds.

They attacked toes, heads, tails—even on their sleeping perches there was no peace. Everything was red with their blood, and we noticed that they had a wild and confused look in their eyes.

We found a description of this disease under the heading "Cannibalism," but the treatment recommended for it, cutting off the beaks, seemed to us cruel and just as senselessly external as putting straitjackets on the insane.

The causes listed for cannibalism were overpopulation of chicken houses, biting insects, and inactivity. None of these applied to our housing and care of chickens.

The most noteworthy thing, however, was that this disease was listed among the deficiency diseases, like rickets, polyneuritis, and the "bent toes" described above, and could be ascribed to a lack of vitamins.

Additional salt was recommended.

Since we had had such good results with our vitamin cure of the ducks, we set up a combined treatment.

To be quite certain that there was no chance that insects were involved, we bathed all the cannibals in warm water to which sulphur and soap had been added, a solution in which no mite can survive. Then we dried the birds, dusted them with louse powder, and disinfected all the poultry houses.

Then, on the advice of a farmer, we gave them two heads of cabbage for vitamin A. At first they rolled these around in the chicken houses as if they were bowling with skulls. Later they pecked into the cabbages and ate some of them, but when they got tired of playing with them they went back to pecking at each other.

We had mixed rice bran, wheat germ, and yeast in granular form into their laying mash and regular feed, and we set aside their corn ration as too "hot," to use the medieval medicine book term. Meanwhile we prepared oat sprouts by letting oats germinate, and we set oats and oat sprouts out for them in big wash basins.

After two days of this cure they were tame again, sociable, intelligent, and ready to live together in peace instead of mauling and pecking each other to death. Everything was in order again, except that I had been jolted and couldn't get away from the strange conclusions that I had to draw from the fact that it had been possible to fight pugnacity, bloodthirstiness, and insanity with vitamins.

And if you let yourself fantasize further, something that is easy to do in farm life, you can spin the thread out and come upon the strange connection between the practical use of yeast, oat sprouts, and wheat germ and the ideas they have stood for: fermenting, sprouting, and germinating, processes that can have a morbidly dangerous meaning, but also simply serve as symbols for growth.

After this report of our successful treatment of animals, their correct and appropriate feeding and housing, it seems to me that it is time to give credit to the USDA so that we don't give the impression that we worked into farm life so quickly by particular industry, ability, and intuition.

We did nothing more than to realize from the beginning that you can't do better than to live with the USDA from cradle to grave in barn, meadows, fields, woods, house, yard, kitchen, and workshop, and that it is only good sense to take this invisible mentor into your house and to get involved in his life.

In a book about the USDA I found the following description of its functions:

> The Department of Agriculture affects the life and living of the American farmer and his family. There is scarcely a phase of farm life which is not dealt with in some way by at least one of the fifty-odd bureaus and agencies in the department. . . . The functions of these branches cover just about everything the farmer has done, is doing, plans to do, or wants to do.
>
> Agencies provide easy, low-interest loans on his farm or future crops. They make cash payments to him for terracing his own field to keep soil from washing away, for building a pond in his pasture, or for applying fertilizer and growing legumes to make the fields produce more.
>
> The bureaus tell the farmer how to grow spinach in his

garden for home use or in the field as a commercial crop, and then they tell him what kind of price he may receive for his peanuts and who may buy them. They regulate the time and place of marketing his crops. They make cash subsidy payments to the dairy farmer from the public treasury when consumers complain that milk is too high, and they solve his labor problem by sending him a farmhand or by installing electricity to operate a milking machine.

They keep thousands of specialists constantly at work seeking new crops, better cropping methods, and means of combating insect pests and crop or livestock diseases. They try to circumvent the hazards of drought, flood, and frost so that production may be increased. If precautions fail and the harvest is lost, those farmers who have insured their crops with the government will receive so many bushels per acre (or its equivalent) from the government warehouses. . . .

The bureaus of the Department of Agriculture help the farmers to grade and market his crops and livestock. If no buyers are available other bureaus are authorized to make crop loans to keep the produce off the market until buyers are at hand, or until the price goes up. They can even buy commodities outright and resell them later at huge financial losses. . . .

Another bureau's job is to study diets and nutrition, advising on these subjects as well as on how to make a chair more comfortable and attractive.

At first we knew little about the functions and scope of the USDA, and our relationship to it could be described as entirely practical. It supplied us with bulletins, tested our soil samples and animals, and gave information in response to questions.

It was evident that it must have many sources of information, that it had laboratories and employed a considerable staff of scientists and agricultural experts who wrote down the results of their research in simple language in bulletins and distributed them.

The study of the development of agriculture in America, a development that continues daily and hourly right under our eyes, is doubtless one of the most interesting and important means to an understanding of the past, present, and future history of America. I can only tell a little of it now, for where I am writing in Europe the material about the history of the USDA is not at hand, and I am no longer in touch with the changes that may have taken place.

However, since the USDA is one of the most significant and important institutions of America, I cannot avoid telling about this powerful support system, this unique institution with which we spent our daily life.

Life with the USDA

It began this way:

When we received the first bulletins from our congressman and learned what information was available, we started to look over the farm and its soil.

We had rented about 193 acres of land. Two-thirds were forested, and one-third was pasture. We decided not to cultivate more than an acre because it was even harder to get hired help during the war than in peacetime.

The ground, except for the piece in front of the house that we kept as lawn, was uncultivated and wild. It was thick with weeds, but it had not been over-farmed, used up, and destroyed, the way the land has been in large sections of America.

I wrote a card to the department of the USDA that is responsible for soil testing and soon received a cylindrical container in which I was supposed to send in a sample of our dirt.

A little while after this was done I received a report on the composition of the soil we intended to cultivate. It also told us what kinds of fertilizers were available, in which places sowing legumes was recommended, and where we should sow millet to drive out the present weeds.

During the war it was hard to get fertilizers, but that suited us because we thought that well-rotted manure should play a larger role on small farms than expensive commercial fertilizers.

109

This correspondence about soil composition took place in the first fall of our arrival on the farm.

In the winter we collected necessary information from the bulletins, as I have already told in the previous chapters, and laid out a systematic plan.

We agreed on the kinds of animals we would get, where we would buy them, which breeds they should be, and what their housing should look like. Then we went on to study feeds.

That is truly a course of study. We learned with astonishment about the many types of nourishment needed by poultry for growing and egg-laying, by goats for milk production, and by pigs for a fattening diet.

There was meal and grain feed for the chicks, young chickens, laying hens, geese, ducks, goats, and pigs. The feed contained corn, wheat, barley, oats, soy beans, alfalfa, bone meal, meat and fish meal, skim milk, sunflower seeds, linseed oil, cod-liver oil, etc. The mixture varied according to the type and age of animal, and its purpose. Carefully compounded mixtures could be bought ready-mixed in the warehouses of the large feed companies under the names: chick feed, strengthening meal for growing chickens, laying meal, fattening meal, scratch feed, milk feed, "manna" for calves, sheep and goat feed, and pig feed. Then there were ground oyster shells (mussel lime), which the laying hens ate to form strong eggshells, and gravel, which all the poultry needed for good digestion, and which varied from the finest to the coarsest according to their age ranges.

In addition we planted alfalfa, soy beans, ladino and red clover, turnips and peas, parsnips, stock beets, and corn for the animals. For ourselves we planted sweet corn, potatoes, and a vegetable garden. We kept a grassy meadow for the chickens, where they promenaded as though in a park, just to throw themselves most of the time on the large manure pile, even though it was heaped up a distance away in the shadow of a barn.

Thinking back, I ask myself why we didn't make ourselves more comfortable, why we didn't simply throw the chickens a little corn, leftovers, and potatoes, let them walk around on the manure and sleep in the goats' shed. Why didn't we feed, house, and treat them as they are treated in countless farm-

110

yards in Europe and still are on many small farms in America?

The question is not so easy to answer.

It was probably because for us farming was not laden with custom and tradition. Our teachers were not our fathers and forefathers or farming neighbors, but the USDA, which rapidly put the results of its scientific experiments to practical uses and distributed these results in commonly understood terms. That meant, since we didn't know the common practices, we had the will and the desire to jump into something quite new and unknown, and were caught up in the excitement of exploration, experimentation, and results.

By following exactly the feed method described above, for example, we could make the moulting period for the chickens very late and short, so that the bad laying time often lasted only two months and didn't begin until December. If we replaced the fattening mash for the young female chickens with the laying meal at the right time, they were already laying at an age of five or six months, and this in the fall when egg prices climb and you can count on a comfortable profit from the proceeds of fall and winter egg production.

The USDA has established on the basis of its statistics and through experiments on its demonstration farms that a farm hen lays 80–86 eggs per year on an average, and that a hen whose breed has been specialized for production, resistance to disease and climate changes, and has been expertly housed and fed, brings a minimum production of 160 eggs in a year and might also produce up to 200 or 250.

It is not only a question of increased production, but also that in America, especially in the country, you are completely on your own. You cannot and dare not count on farmhands or household help—it is rare and expensive. In order to cope with all parts of the unfamiliar work, we had to develop a method cut to fit a way of life which was new to us. The cutting is, for the most part, performed in America by the USDA, but you must of course sew up the pieces for yourself.

That the USDA concerned itself with new farm machinery, with new varieties of corn and wheat, that it battled against animal and plant diseases, that it explored the effect of light on plants, that it developed hormone preparations against infertility and for increased milk production in animals, that it recommended scientific fertilization, that it employed chemical preparations, bacteria, and insects against insect pests, that it undertook every kind of soil improvement, and in all of these areas initiated and maintained an immense research operation, did not seem so amazing to me as the fact that it concerned itself with the smallest details of farming, with apparently immaterial bits of housekeeping, and with the primitive aspects of daily farm life.

What sort of institution could it be that concerns itself with the production of cotton, tobacco, corn, wheat, cattle, wood, and all the other gigantic factors of farming that play a decisive role in world production, and at the same time counts the steps a housewife takes in her kitchen in order to discover what technical equipment may spare her two-thirds of these steps?

What sort of a government bureau would describe for farmers how to upholster chairs, which wallpapers and pictures they should select, how they can update hats and the best way to clean their teeth, what kind of colored house aprons make you happy, how you can recognize antique early American furniture, what you can make for Christmas presents, which neckties to buy, and how you can develop an attractive, comfortable appearance through correct posture?

On the basis of these questions it seemed to me to be worth knowing how this remarkable Department of Agriculture was established, how far-flung its functions are, and how high the cost is to keep this apparatus in motion.

In America one quickly becomes accustomed to statistics and astronomical figures.

The distances, areas, and the overview of huge plains are so large and hyperdimensional that in the beginning you find yourself wishing to count time in light-years. Gradually you learn to understand the inclination of Americans for huge numbers and the feeling of space, and at the same time you must not forget that many of them came from the narrow confines of Europe.

However, when I found the dimensions of the USDA for the first time, it took my breath away for a moment.

I read that the USDA has eighty thousand permanent employees and distributes more than a billion dollars a year to six million farming operations.

112

I found a map which showed where the fifty main experiment stations are located, with countless little dots for smaller laboratories and experiment stations. In addition there are the many offices in the 3,074 counties of the states which distribute the results of research in the form of brochures and have a direct relationship with the individual farmer.

The functions of the USDA include three main areas: administration, research, and information. They deal with all the branches of agriculture from road building, farm credit, and market prices through information about insects to household economy, as I have already mentioned in other chapters.

The USDA was first represented in the Cabinet as the independent Department of Agriculture in 1889. The Cabinet already had the Secretaries of State, the Interior, War, the Navy, and the Treasury, the Postmaster General, and Attorney General. It was enlarged in 1913 by the addition of the Secretaries of Trade and Labor.

The USDA began in the Patent Office.

The Patent Office received experimental seeds sent from all over the world.

> Now there was at that time a Patent Commissioner by the name of Mr. Henry L. Ellsworth, who was a farmer from Connecticut. In his capacity as Commissioner of the Patent Office, and at the same time as authorized agent for Indian Affairs, he made tours of inspection through the entire country. Mr. Ellsworth, it is reported, was deeply impressed by the agricultural possibilities of the western prairies, and also by the ignorance and bitter poverty of the settlers there. He was convinced that they could be helped by the development of better tools and seed adapted to the climate and soil. He saw the need for this as so pressing that, on his own authority without asking Congress, he had seeds and plants distributed to the farmers throughout the country, and especially in the West.

Under this energetic Mr. Ellsworth, the Patent Office became a separate office on July 4, 1836, and only three years later this new office was granted one thousand dollars for scientific agricultural purposes.

The year 1862, under President Lincoln, saw three important pieces of legislation for agriculture. On May 15, 1862, a Commissioner of Agriculture was named, but without a seat in the Cabinet. At the same time, however, a separate Department of Agriculture was established, and the responsibilities of this department were outlined. It should assemble worthwhile practical agricultural information; introduce useful plants, seeds, and animals; answer farmers' questions; and choose themes for publications according to their inquiries. It was to study and experiment with tools, soil development, seeds, fertilizers, and animals; undertake chemical analysis of soils, grains, fruits, vegetables, and fertilizers and publish the results; collect botanical and insect information; and furnish libraries and museums.

Five days after the establishment of the Bureau of Agriculture, the Homestead Act was passed on the twentieth of May. This meant that every man and woman over twenty-one years of age could claim 160 acres of land from the public domain, the available government property. After five years of working and improving it, they could register as owners of the land. The statute held for Americans or foreigners who wished to become American citizens. The only persons excluded from this distribution were those who had fought against the United States.

On July 2, 1862, the Land Grant College Act was passed. This put eleven million acres of public land at the disposal of the state universities. From the proceeds of these, the individual states were to endow their agricultural colleges.

With the passage of these three statutes, agriculture was placed on a foundation of assured support and information.

In the Bureau of Agriculture one division followed another: the Food and Drug Administration, Bureau of Animal Industry, Office of Experimental Stations, Weather Bureau, and so on.

After the USDA became a cabinet-level bureau, bureaus of Soils, Plant Industry, Forestry, Chemistry, Entomology, Office of Public Roads, etc., were added.

The history of agriculture and the establishment of the USDA is a remarkable and interesting conglomeration of history, science, and politics, but at the same time a document of perseverance, endurance, and arrogance, of the sins, virtues,

114

indifference, and unbreakable spirit of mankind.

One can only understand the importance and the present size of the USDA if one recognizes a few fundamentals of the agricultural history of America.

A university professor from Tennessee wrote the following concise description of the early farmers in America:

> The first farmers in America had to battle with countless great obstacles: with the natural wilderness, the attacks of Indians and wild animals on their herds, with the difficulty of obtaining tools and seeds, with the necessity of becoming familiar with climate and soil which was completely different from what they were accustomed to at home. The first settlers were limited to the most primitive methods. They felled and burnt the smaller trees and the underbrush. Then they plowed the earth superficially with home-made plows and cultivated corn and tobacco with wooden rakes. The settlers accepted the harvest that nature gave them without thinking and used it wastefully. They cultivated the soil until it was exhausted and useless. Then they pushed on with their families and cleared new tracts of land. As long as there was immeasurable land available, no attention was paid to the conservation and fertility of the soil. America was such a wide and fruitful country that men used it this way for more than a hundred years before they discovered that there were limits even to the most productive land.

At that time, when some notion of these limits began to dawn, it appears to have occurred to people to plant the seed of the USDA in this barren, unfruitful soil. It is no wonder that in our time the starting point of all agricultural problems for the USDA lies in the question of how we can make productive again the enormous areas of America which were destroyed through wantonness, speculation, and ignorance.

You have to picture the situation clearly. For centuries countless Europeans came from their poor little fields and went into debt to set up farms in this immense land. They enacted a story like the sagas and old legends.

They had to fight their way through impenetrable forests and frightful dangers, endure heat, storms, and cold, live in caves or primitive log cabins and go through all the stages and tests of courage. If they didn't perish on the way, they could succeed in amassing great fortunes.

However, these experiences and tests of courage changed the basic character of these Europeans and awoke in them an unquenchable desire for further wandering. As they hurried on from place to place, the tests they had to endure turned into adventures. They became accustomed to a nomadic, unstable way of life. They believed that limitless profits could be taken out without returning anything. They farmed wastefully without thinking about it because they forgot that everything needed to be conserved and cared for, including the soil if it is going to produce harvests.

The USDA has returned about fifty million acres of land to productivity in recent years. That is only a tenth of the area that had been ruined by erosion and turned into barren, unfruitful land.

In the yearbook of the USDA for 1943–1947, I read:

> Education and research go together. Even more important than mere teaching of technology is the teaching of the scientific method. Its cultural values perhaps exceed its purely practical ones, great as these are. The methods of science are those of democracy. Each citizen needs to learn how to use science himself and not rely wholly on the expert.
>
> Nowhere is this more important than on farms. It would be a sorry day for democracy if farmers generally turned to experts to make decisions for them. They need to learn from scientists, of course. It is the job of scientists to give them information in ways they can understand and use, and to work with them. It is definitely not one of doing the job of farming for the farmer.
>
> The lag in time between the development of new knowledge and techniques through research and their use by farmers is too great. This is especially true of those things that require a considerable change in the farming system for realization of the benefits. The use of hybrid seed corn spread quickly because no change in practice was necessary other than the source of seed. But the substitution of new pasture and feed crops for cotton on soils better adapted to them may require a complete change in the farming system. Such changes come too slowly. . . .

> Each step is vital to the others. . . . None should be
> allowed to lag. Nor should the time of peace be wasted.

In another place in the same article, we can read: "We know that science is bound to remake the world even faster, either in an orderly and not too slow a way, or in a series of catastrophes. This very fact of change gives us another chance to solve the problems that lead to war. Any solution will recognize that because farm science touches all our lives, a good world will be one where farm science is strong and alert.

"What some of us do not realize, perhaps, is that science can make abundance physically possible. That is important, because we should know by now that no group can be secure while others are without confidence and hope."

This means that the USDA wants to educate farmers to be independent, to use the results of research experiments. It means that the USDA has been intended from its beginning to be a source of knowledge in understandable terms for solving practical everyday problems, a collector and distributor of common resources.

This means that, while the USDA is concerned with the smallest and most trifling details of present living, it is prepared to teach people what they need to know for a new world. It shows that the USDA is an attempt to take action before it is too late, a manifestation of the will to correct the mistakes of the past, an expression of well-timed concern about present conditions and of a determination to build a better future.

Thus the USDA *could* hold the key to keeping peace, preventing hunger, and preserving life.

Marie

One evening we were sitting at the table with the children, who were spending a short school vacation with us. We were all in that pleasant mood that makes life seem easy and unburdened and brings laughter over small and insignificant things.

The cheerfulness that evening came, on the one hand, from the practical fact that Zuck had sold an article to a magazine and that some money had come into the house again. On the other hand, it was because Michi, whose specialties were baking, sewing, and knitting, had decided to produce some genuine Mardi gras fritters. This was a daring enterprise, since it was February and the temperature outside had plunged to thirty-five degrees below zero.

First she had locked us all out of the kitchen so that no draft could disturb the rising dough. Then she let us back in only when the fritters were swimming in hot fat and the table was festively set. In the kitchen it was steaming hot. Frost pictures on the kitchen windows shut out the frozen landscape which lay ominously around the house. Half of the fritters were lying on paper towels, tender and light brown, each with a yellow stripe around the middle like an equator. They were ready to be moved to the warmed plates, while the rest of the fritters still spluttered in the fat.

We sat down at the table, complimented Michi, praised her fritters, and settled into that state of undemanding comfort that can occur either suddenly or arises slowly from warmth, delicious food, and a feeling of belonging in the family or among friends.

The children asked Zuck if he would build a big fire in the living room fireplace and brew up some "hot buttered rum," a pleasant kind of punch for polar regions that is made of rum and sweet cider. It is always served in cups, and you put a small piece of butter in each cup, which melts on the surface of the hot drink and enhances, rather than decreases, the rum taste.

First Zuck had to go to the barn to get gigantic logs to fill the stove in the living room. Then he brought in a couple of birch logs to lay on the fire in the open fireplace.

When he went through the kitchen with the second load of wood, Michi said suddenly, as a dark shadow fell over her face, "Will there ever be a time in our lives again when we don't have to jump up right after a meal to stack mountains of dishes and wash and dry them, when you don't have to carry wood, shake down coals, and build fires, when the kitchen is not papered with all these frightful lists telling what to do and when, without any prospect of ever catching up with all the work, without any hope of finishing?"

Zuck paused a moment in the kitchen. He couldn't shrug his shoulders because the wood he was carrying in his arms was too heavy, but there was shoulder shrugging in his tone as he said, "I don't know whether things will ever change, but perhaps it is all right the way it is. . ."

"It is not all right this way," I said, "especially for a man who has something more important in his head, who has other work to do than heating, milking, and cleaning pigpens."

"Bitterness will get you nowhere," cried Winnetou, who had learned this bitter motto in school. "I'll feed the cats now while you wash the dishes. Then I'll help dry while you make the rum. When we are done we'll have room for a couple more fritters."

Half an hour later we sat in the living room. The children lay in front of the fireplace and stretched their feet toward the open fire.

A mountain of Mardi gras fritters stood on the table. It smelled of wood smoke and rum punch, of New Year's Eve and Mardi gras, and we all felt a combination of being at home and shut away from the outside world, a feeling you can never have when neighbors are near and easy to reach. We spoke dreamily, a little tired, accepting our fate and ready to find again in our situation the humor that we had lost for a moment.

Again and again we came back to the theme of "hired help" and looked at it from all angles.

The children reminisced about the good old days when we had four servants and their nanny would encourage them, in spite of our disapproval, to ring for the chamber maid, even if all they wanted was a glass of water.

We spoke of the lives of our servants, in which we had been much interested and often deeply involved. We got out the letters that they had written us, at great danger to themselves, after Hitler seized power. They were examples of "noble simplicity and quiet greatness."

We spoke of the concept of service and the related idea of master, of the calling of the servant or waitress, of the situation of being waited on, and of work itself.

We found many examples from our past European and our present American life, but we found no satisfactory solution for the future and saw only the impossible amount of work ahead of us, too much to ever catch up with.

In the course of the evening, I said to Michi, "It makes me think of a funny story. It is silly, but really true. In New York, two immigrants from Austria met each other on the street. 'Isn't it wonderful,' said one, 'all the things there are here in America! We couldn't have dreamed of it. Everywhere electric refrigerators, washing machines, singing tea kettles, automatic can openers!' 'Yes, that is all very nice,' interrupted the other with a deep sigh, 'but I really liked having Marie better.' "

Back here in Europe, where I am writing, I often have to think back to that Mardi gras fritter evening and our talk.

I am amazed and deeply impressed by the number of Maries, Annas, Rosas, Mizzis, Kathis, Friedas, and Ellas that are still available. They clean rooms, make beds, set tables, cook, serve the food, wash the dishes, and are always there to do burdensome, dirty, constant, endless work for others.

Naturally, wealthy Americans do have servants, but just the fact that a very small percentage of New York apartments have rooms for servants shows how small the number of live-in servants must be.

The normal situation for a city dweller is to have a woman, black or white, who comes in for a couple of hours two or three times a week.

The hourly wages are high, but there is seldom a personal relationship. In wartime, the connection was so loose that you never knew whether the help that had cleaned so cheerfully on Monday would not stay away on Thursday without notice or goodbye. On the other hand, you had no responsibility to them and could dismiss them at any time without giving a reason.

At the beginning I found it frightening when a girl suddenly packed up her things and departed forever with no real reason and after five years of service. Or when a family moved to another state and suddenly told their maid who had served them faithfully for years that she would no longer be needed. Slowly I began to realize that in America it was not a matter of obligations, as they existed in the better and worse sense in Europe, but of work, a "job" like any other that was done in the most practical and unemotional way possible.

In Vermont matters were even more difficult, and in war-time almost impossible.

By nature Vermonters make poor servants. They can decide of course to help someone, but you must not take this help for granted or as something to be bought. The wages they demand for their work are relatively low because that increases their sense of independence.

Once a friend of ours was looking desperately for a boy to mow the grass.

After a long search one finally came and was asked how much he wanted per hour.

"Fifty cents per hour," he answered, "but sixty, if you try to tell me how to do it."

In the first year we were lucky.

That year a Vermont woman from the village came to us three times a week for four hours. She had been a teacher. Now she was widowed, had two children, and could only do domestic work.

She was pretty, quiet, and pleasant. We were glad to have

her at our table, and we gave her no dirty or unpleasant tasks to do. Also she was a news reporter for the weekly newspaper, and while she was with us you could read much about our family in the news, for example when the children were home on vacation, whom we visited, and who came to visit us.

After a year she moved to the city, and then we had to get along for two years without any household help. That was hard since the house had ten rooms, with the living room a large hall and the kitchen the size of a dance floor.

Only in the fall of 1944 were we able to get the help of a farmer's daughter. She came twice a week, but left in the spring of 1946 to get married.

The other farmers had just as much trouble as we did. They had an unbelievable amount of work to do without the corresponding help. There was a farm with fifteen hundred chickens, eight cows, twelve young stock, four pigs, thirty acres of cultivated land, and five hundred sugar maples from which the sap had to be collected and boiled down. The farmer had to take care of all this work with the help of one old man, and perhaps in summer one or two hired boys to help with the field work. Another farmer had to milk his sixty cows twice a day for months with the help of a young boy. Another took care of his sixteen cows himself and worked besides as a woodcutter.

Even these few examples show how agricultural machinery for the field, electric milking machines in the barn, and a hundred and one small appliances in the house are essential to help the overworked farmer and his wife cope to some extent with the enormous load of work.

Under these circumstances it was also impossible to ask friendly farmers for help, since they had almost more than they could do with their own work.

We could write a book about the hired boys, boys between twelve and seventeen years old, who went through our house in a colorful procession, each with his own individual and amazing traits, and never there when we wanted them. They had to leave the house at seven o'clock in the morning and came home in the evening at will, and asked every day as if for the first time what we wanted them to do, though their work was laid out in great detail.

Feeding them was no problem. If they were country boys,

they usually ate only potatoes, beans, frankfurters, and sausage. That was all, and they made up for the missing vitamins with cigarette smoking.

Two of them who looked, in spite of the fresh country air, as if they were suffering from tuberculosis, scurvy, and starvation were taken into the army even with their miserable appearance. There they were forced to eat steaks, vegetables, and fruit, and under this treatment grew into healthy young giants in spite of themselves. When one of them came back from Japan six months after the war and greeted me on the street, I didn't recognize him.

Since we had gotten used to the peculiarities of our animals, we adjusted to the ways of our hired boys, although I dreaded Saturdays when they were out of school and we had to put up with them all day long. Now that the new methods of educating the young have spread to the country, and the poor children are allowed to do and leave undone what they want to without being warned away from things that are wrong and led towards what is right by helpful adults, they are helpless in the face of a pseudo-freedom in which they don't know where to turn.

Children sail on wild, unfamiliar seas in boats without rudder or compass, or run aground on sandbanks. As a natural consequence they direct their anger and frustration against the adults who have given them the great and tempting gift of the boat but forgotten to provide it with rudder and compass.

It was impressed on the children, however, that they are children and therefore, like fools, can be excused everything.

Once I came home to find that our thirteen-year-old hired boy had amused himself in our absence by building a fire on the *top* of the wood stove, feeding it with such generous amounts of wood that the whole kitchen was filled with smoke and glowing pieces of wood had scattered onto the floor. When I quickly extinguished the fire on the stove with water and tamped out the glowing coals on the floor, he watched my hurried actions with folded arms.

I got angry and told him that he could have been responsible for setting the whole house on fire with his play, at which he looked at me visibly surprised and replied as if insulted, "What do you expect of me—I'm just a kid."

This statement didn't lack a certain humor, but from then on it was uncanny to me all that he could blame on his childhood and childishness, and I only wanted to get him out of our house as soon as possible.

Our hired boys never stayed long. Some came to us only for Christmas and summer vacations. But in spite of their many problems it was always hard for us when they left, and we had to do all the work again ourselves.

The length of stay often depended on an order from Sears and Roebuck. According to whether they had ordered a pair of jeans or a gun, I could figure out from the catalog how much they would have to pay for it. Then I divided the pay that they got from us by the sum of the things ordered from Sears and Roebuck and could see clearly how many weeks they would still be with us. If I look back and count, there were really only ten hired boys in all who stayed with us for shorter or longer periods, but to me it seemed like a whole company because they were so different from each other and it cost so much effort and adjustment to get along with them.

Some of them came from Vermont, some from the city, and three were immigrants.

I had a particularly difficult time with one of them. He was a lively, bright boy from Austria who had picked up all the garbage from the social trash bins of America with incredible speed, had gobbled it down, and digested it badly.

I found him one morning in our living room, his hat on his head, his feet on the table, Zuck's whiskey bottle next to him on the floor, with playing cards in his hands. He had the radio turned on to its highest volume and was playing poker with himself, stopping now and then to spit into the fireplace.

I went and stood in front of him, regarding him with disgust. "Are you quite sure," I asked him cheerfully, "that people will believe that you are a born American because you put your feet on the table, spit, swear, drink, and talk common American slang? I warn you, Americans can smell out fakes. Perhaps you should take a different American type as a pattern, one that would suit you better and be more convincing."

Among all these hired boys there was one who sometimes disappeared but kept returning. We had gotten to know him in our summer visits to the area when he was thirteen. When he

was fifteen he came to us on the farm, and so we called him our first boy.

He came from a family with many children. His father was a woodcutter and day laborer, and when he came to us he was as much a beginner in farming as we.

He was very handsome, had nice manners, didn't curse, drink, or smoke. Nor did he pin up pictures of half naked movie actresses on the walls of the chicken houses, or lie stretched out on our sofa in the pose of Madame Recamier. He didn't kiss our pigs on the snout, tease little animals, or try to use empty jam jars as toilets. He avoided starting fires and ate almost everything we set before him. He was not a model boy, but his faults were balanced out by his good will and childlike simplicity.

Most of all he wanted not to be a child. Rather he was driven by a serious desire to be grown up, and therefore ordered suits from Sears and Roebuck whose cut and color would have been just as suitable for grown men.

The fine, clean shirts that he wore Sundays made such a contrast in color to his neck and ears that I urged him, whenever possible, to take a bath on Saturday night, a job that he felt was the lowest and dirtiest possible. On one Saturday he was going around with a sullen and gloomy face, and when Zuck asked him what was wrong, he said sadly and resentfully, "She wants me to take a bath again."

For his sixteenth birthday I gave him bath salts and thus made bathing so attractive that he spent hours in the water and I had to knock on the door with the reminder, "Don't forget to wash."

A striving to get ahead filled everything he did. The most trying thing for us was his fierce urge for education, together with the high opinion he had formed of us and forced us to live up to.

Zuck would avoid his questions by disappearing into his room in the evenings where he sometimes made attempts to write.

But I had to stay in the kitchen and answer his questions without batting an eyelash, always trying to maintain his illusions about my knowledge.

Usually they were just information questions, but some-

126

times they had to do with problems that took deeper digging.

One night he came home in a wild snowstorm, threw his backpack, cap, and coat on the kitchen floor and called out to me, busy in the midst of cooking something, "Who was right, Elizabeth or Mary Stuart?"

Experienced as I was by now, I looked first for the source of this question and learned that he had just finished reading "Stiffn Swig."

After I learned slowly and by having it spelled out that Stiffn Swig was Stefan Zweig, and that the question came from reading his book about Mary Stuart, I had the basis for our discussion. When Zuck came into the kitchen a while later, the goats had not been milked, the pigs and fowl not fed, but there had been a certain understanding reached about the significance of Queen Elizabeth.

After that he busied himself for some time with English and French history. One fine fall day, as we sat outside sorting the potatoes we had dug for winter storage, he suddenly said thoughtfully, "After the war I think I'll rent a room in the Versailles palace."

"I don't think they rent rooms," I said, "but perhaps you could be a tour guide there. For that you must take an extra course in French and learn all you can about the French kings. And don't forget Napoleon."

After that I lived with Pompadour, Marie Antoinette, Beauharnais, and Fouche, but that was all right since it was just at the time when we were hanging ears of corn up to dry in the house and barns, and discussions could be easily conducted from the ladder.

It was more difficult to answer questions about the present. These took in a wide spate of themes. The simplest were perhaps, "How would you act if the Japanese came? Why isn't Hitler removed by the people and someone else elected? Are you related to the Hapsburgs, and why not? Is it true that the farmers in Europe live in the same room with their animals?"

One of the most difficult questions came up while we were boiling down maple syrup.

Suddenly he asked as if lost in thought, "Would you stand up if Mrs. Roosevelt came into the kitchen?"

"Yes," I said, with my attention on the bubbling syrup, "of

course I would stand up."

"Would you stand up because she is the wife of the president?"

"Yes," I said absentmindedly, and I stuck the thermometer into the syrup.

"You shouldn't do that," he said, shaking his head. "You are just as good as Mrs. Roosevelt. . ."

Just at this moment three pans of maple syrup were done and had to be removed from the stove immediately. This gave me time to think about how I could extricate myself from the accusation that I was a servile European.

When the next pans had been filled with cold sap and set on the stove, I said casually, "But Mrs. Roosevelt would still be my guest, and you have to stand up for guests." That satisfied him.

Because of his occupation with historical questions and current problems he fell behind in mathematics and told us one fine day that he would have to stay away for months so that he wouldn't be kept back in school. For similar reasons he had often disappeared for weeks in the past.

Before his departure he rearranged the stone cellar of our house and transformed it into a magnificent bar for guests who might want to take refuge in our cool cellar on hot summer days. He found an enormous wooden table and two benches in the barn. He put stone jugs on barrels with candles in the jug necks, and he stuck the one sad little electric light bulb into a barn lantern. As a final touch he hung a gun from the Civil War like the sword of Damocles over the table. I didn't want to interfere with this romantic project.

Then he went to his mathematics and we didn't see him again for six months. One day I met him on the street in front of a store.

He helped me to put the packages I was carrying into the car. Then he climbed into the front seat and said, "I can come to you for only four months. Then I'll be eighteen and must sign up."

In these last months he didn't talk or ask questions so much because he was playing the phonograph day and night and had spent all his extra money before he came to us on Beethoven, Mozart, Brahms, and Tchaikovsky records.

"It doesn't make sense to spend more money for suits and shirts," he explained to me, "when I am going to have to wear a uniform. But this is something for the future. The records will be here when I come home again."

With these words he put on the "Kleine Nachtmusik" for the 150th time and stretched himself out comfortably in Zuck's wing chair, which stood next to the phonograph in the living room.

"Beautiful music," he said. "I like it. I suppose you know it all already from over there?"

By the time he had to go into the army, the war was fortunately over. After a long time I received a letter from him from Alaska.

"The winter is milder here than in Vermont," he wrote. "I am sitting here with seven other fellows on a little island. It is very boring, but I have eight Shakespeare plays with me and am learning the roles by heart. Perhaps I will be an actor, or do you think I should be an architect instead? We are all bad cooks, but we have lots of meat and chicken. Please send me the recipe for chicken paprika as soon as you can."

That was our first boy.

He was not the rule, nor were many of our hired boys typical of the hired boys you could get.

The hard-working and dependable ones, who had the makings of excellent future farmers, were mostly going to agricultural colleges or working on big farms and unavailable to us. So all year we had to do all the work ourselves with only a very little help, work that was made up of endless little tasks, all spelled out on the "frightful lists" in the kitchen.

When we saw Henndorf again for the first time and spent two days there in our old house, I wrote to Michi,

> Everything is changed and quite different from what we had imagined.
>
> But Ederin is here and keeps the house clean, and Anna has come for a visit and does the cooking, and another maid is here who has been hired by our landlady.
>
> The house itself is practically unchanged, even though all the silver, clothing, and linens were stolen from it. The main room is the same: we eat from handpainted china and drink from beautiful Tyrolean glasses. The kitchen

stove is filled by Ederin, Anna cooks, and the new maid serves.

The table is cleared—we hear the rattle of dishes in the kitchen—the wood crackles in the stove. We sit here and don't lift a finger. We carry on conversations with the guests, but we catch ourselves listening to the noises in the kitchen with one ear. Suddenly we realize that we no longer have the innocence of the upper class, that with every sound the individual links in the chain of the work pass before our eyes.

The next day I went up to the attic with Ederin. She opened up chests, boxes, and trunks, and I found books, pictures, letters, and your playthings.

It was as if we had lived in the house a hundred years ago, and I was poking around in my own inheritance.

Henndorf was not destroyed, and Salzburg suffered little damage. It doesn't look like most of the German cities. . .

But, just think, even in the destroyed cities there is still a good supply of Maries, Rosas, and Friedas. There it is uncanny to see how they put together tablecloths with a thousand mends, wash dishes with rags, use the ragged remains of underwear for dust cloths, how they cook the porridge sullenly and serve the pea soup in a friendly way. If you could see how they set out the chipped china just like the finest Meissen ware, and bring on something that looks like shoe polish as if it were crêpes suzette, if you could see how they listen and nod, carry on and off, go back and forth, if you could hear them complain about the bad times, as unchanged as if they were still living in the good old days, you would think you had been spirited away into a ghostly land.

And if you watched the upper class, the upper class with whom you are sitting at the table, who often live in greater wretchedness and more bitter poverty than their servant girls because these may have farming relatives somewhere in the country, if you saw how they no longer have any of the attributes of the upper class, you would feel the icy wind of death even as you sit here alive.

I am happy about every Marie that is still here, even when I know that she is only a symbol. I am thankful for every Rosa who still serves me.

But I know that the era of Maries is past. Perhaps they

130

will in my lifetime go to the factories or find other work, as in America, and even when they stay in housework they will no longer be the Maries they were.

But I can't be afraid of that because we learned in America to turn our attention to everyday matters, and we could see that a time would come when imagination and technology would make the way easy, the time short, and the effort small that one has to spend on the work of daily living.

The *Standard*

In this book nothing is made up.

For that reason I have told a lot about our animals, but only a little about our neighbors, friends, and other people. This did not occur by accident, but on purpose.

I am reminded of a story that I once read a long time ago in the book *Three Men in a Boat* by Jerome Jerome.

As the three friends are bathing one morning on their boat, it happens that a shirt falls in the water. All three break out laughing, and their hilarity knows no bounds. But suddenly one of the three notices that it is his shirt that is floating on the water, stops laughing, and becomes angry and abusive. That is it exactly . . .

In this book then nothing is made up, and it will go hard with me if anyone finds his own shirt floating in it. . . . However, since I want to tell something of those with whom we lived and might live again, I have looked for a way and found the best means in the weekly newspaper that played such a significant role in our farm life.

The newspaper is an establishment that belongs to rural life, like Sears and Roebuck and the USDA. One can learn from it what is happening in our community and in neighboring communities, who is visiting whom, who is getting married, when people are sick or die or recover, what they buy and sell, how they celebrate their holidays, what destruction the weather has caused, how things are going in school, in the woods, on the streets, in prison, and in politics.

132

It is not a family paper. It is not an agricultural newspaper. It is a unique phenomenon, a community newspaper in which the members of the community are the actors and purely personal contact is established.

In the United States there are 4,127 community newspapers of this sort.

Our weekly newspaper has its office in the town of Woodstock, which has 1,325 inhabitants, seven churches, fifty businesses, three doctors, two dentists, five lawyers, and no factories.

Seventeen communities from the surrounding area send in their village news weekly to the newspaper; five communities send it in only occasionally.

The newspaper has 1,750 subscribers who pay the yearly subscription price of $2.50. All of these precise figures I took from a letter from the publisher of our community newspaper. I wrote to him from Switzerland and asked him to give me a few facts about the paper, and he answered by return mail.

"Our weekly newspaper," he wrote, "was founded in 1853 as a temperance paper and battled against the production, sale, and use of alcoholic beverages. In those times many newspapers were established as a means of battling or crusading against something. Newspapers first appeared in America in the cities. In the rural communities the newspapers appeared first as by-products of the book publishers. They contained domestic and foreign political news, because rural political activity was carried on through discussions in the store, after church, and at times when people were working together. However, it often happened that the newspapers from the cities arrived too late or not at all, and so the rural population began to turn more and more to local papers to give them desired information.

"From this you can see," the publisher wrote further, "that our community newspaper has changed greatly in the course of time, and that it is a product of the evolution caused by the changing needs of the local population." He closed his letter with the news that they had had and were still having a hard winter, and that they hoped that I would enjoy my Swiss stay and come home soon.

Our weekly newspaper is called the *Vermont Standard*. The

word "Standard" — many newspapers have that name in America — includes many meanings: plumb-line, steadiness, measure, model, value, example, perfection, emblem.

Every week the following explanation appears under the name of the publisher:

"The *Standard* aims to serve the best interests of Woodstock and Windsor County, to present unprejudiced each week's news in a clean, conservative manner, ever respecting the rights of the citizens in the territory it covers. This, we believe, will make it worthy of its readers' confidence."

The paper appears every Thursday, and the local reports in it often affected our lives directly.

We read, for example:

"Mr. and Mrs. Huron Huntoon have returned from Montpelier, where they attended the wedding of Miss Ramona Nelson to Wayne Peltier. Mrs. Huron Huntoon is the sister of the bride. The groom returned from Japan two months ago, where he was stationed with the Marines. They will live in Montpelier."

There went my hope of getting Ramona Nelson as household help, and I had to congratulate them on their marriage with a few bittersweet lines.

A truly frightening announcement was the short notice:

"Bob Russel and Merlin Kennefik have the measles."

I had scarcely read this when I rushed to the drug store to acquire a fever thermometer, gargle, and aspirin for our hired boy. Then I watched him the entire evening after his return to us for signs of a red face and glazed eyes, because he was the best friend of Merlin Kennefik.

Zuck's forehead wrinkled into deep worry lines when he found this item:

"Otis Totmann lost his big toe while cutting wood and had to go to the hospital."

What will happen to the wood that is still lying in the woods and must be brought in before winter? How long would the hospitalization be for a big toe? Will he still be able to bring in the wood on time?

That will be a big piece of work. Zuck will help with piling the wood, and it is disquieting to watch the men at it. When the firewood has reached a height of sixteen feet, the men piling it balance like rope dancers on the pieces of wood. You know

134

that a mislaid piece can bring everything tumbling down. And still they pile on more, higher and higher—no, I was not happy to have Zuck take part in that work.

Once, when they were stacking wood, and I was watching resignedly with clenched teeth, a lumberjack stopped—after he had handed up a large birch log to Zuck—shrugged his shoulders, and remarked to me without taking his pipe out of his mouth:

"One makes it, the other doesn't."

This item looked harmless: "Supper in the community house for the members of the Grange. Clam chowder, frankfurters, salad, cake, and cocoa will be served. Please be there Friday evening promptly at eight o'clock." However, it reminded me that I was on this time and had to bring the salad.

In the same issue I read: "The party which was to take place last Saturday in W. had to be cancelled because of frozen pipes in the house where it was to be held. We hope that the damage will be repaired by next Saturday."

"That doesn't look good," I thought. "First it is so cold that the pipes freeze. Then the great snowfall comes on top of that. And then the Grange evening comes, and I see myself tramping through the woods with the huge salad bowl in my arms and have to watch out so that the heavy snow doesn't fall off the trees into my salad bowl. And then I can stand and wait on the street corner until the postmistress comes and takes the salad bowl. I would like to go to the Grange. It can often be very cheerful with the farmers, and I could see people again. It is already the third week that we have been besieged by snow and ice and marooned as if we were in a mountain hut."

And, after dwelling on these dismal thoughts, I am comforted by finding my negative feelings about winter expressed in print.

> The days of melancholy are back again. We are always melancholy after the first real snowfall, and the more it snows, just so much more do we succumb to a peevish resignation. Every fall, when Thanksgiving draws near and the ground still lies brown and green before us, the wild, senseless hope comes over us that the climate could have changed, and in this year no snow, no snow at all, will fall.
>
> And then the snow comes.

And then these amazing creatures, the tourists and skiers, come storming into our office and exclaim with sparkling eyes and rosy cheeks how wonderful the snow is. We don't understand them, because we only go outside when we absolutely must. To avoid wet feet and inflammation of the lungs we are forced to add twenty to thirty extra pounds of clothing on our feet, and tramp with this weight, panting and wheezing, through the snow without so much as a glance at our surroundings. If we don't go on foot, we have a struggle with the car. If we leave the chains off, the car won't even come out of the garage, but if we have carefully put on the chains, the main streets are suddenly free of snow, and we rattle along like a reaping machine. . . . So much for snow.

After such an outburst one feels easier, and one turns gladly to the mild report of a girl from the community of Prosper, who writes:

"Today is Sunday, the 20th of April, and it snowed all day long. In addition, this is the third snowstorm which we have had to endure in the last five days. One could lose hope, and it is hard for the birds, whom hopefully no one forgets to feed."

The wise people fled before winter:

"And our readers who are basking in Florida's sunshine or live in comfortable winter quarters in Boston or New York, and are in pleasant temperatures, pleased that they have run away from the less pleasant season in Vermont, demand of us that we print more weather reports. We have the understandable impression that these shirkers only want to read our weather reports so that they can write to us: Ha, ha, wouldn't you rather be here with us?"

Among those fleeing the winter was once even our excellent Mrs. Perkins. We read:

"Mrs. Dwaine Perkins has gone by car to Texas with her friend Miss Marjorie Patenaude to celebrate her eightieth birthday there."

By another newspaper notice that ran, "Mrs. Ralph Potter and Mrs. Glenn Benedict visited Mrs. Elie Titcomb on Sunday . . . ," I learned that Mrs. Titcomb had returned home. I called her up and heard from her that Mrs. Perkins did not care for Texas because the turkeys there were disappointing—

the Vermont turkeys were much tastier.

Mrs. Perkins doubtless left right after the big lumberjacks' celebration, which takes place every year in late fall at the town hall. It can storm, blow, and rain then, but we have never missed this event.

Great tree trunks stand in front of the town hall, driven a yard deep in the earth, and powerful lumberjacks stand by the trees and wait for the signal to compete in felling the trees with their axes. Blow follows blow until one tree after another falls. Roger wins, and his nine children who are sitting on the huge lumber wagon add their voices proudly to the murmur of applause. His wife waves to him and then disappears into the darkness with her tenth child to nurse it. Meanwhile the competition continues as the giant logs are sawed through, and this time young Campbell is the winner.

Then it is the women's turn. A piece of tree trunk too big to fit in the highest and widest fireplace must be cut through with a two-person saw.

Now our Mrs. Perkins walks onto the scene, seventy-nine years old, and saws with Miss Patenaude, who is only seventy-six years old. And while they are sawing, precisely and powerfully, you catch a vision of the age of the pioneers. When they win and receive the first prize, you realize why women in America are not inferior to men. What wonderful things are the American celebrations!

In the beginning we paid no attention to the celebrations because they had nothing of the lively peasant quality we knew. They portrayed life directly, truthfully, not in symbols.

I am not speaking here of the occasions that you can find described in the big newspapers that are celebrated by so-called society and are as frivolous, embarrassing, and hazardous as the "parties" of Queen Marie Antoinette, which led in a straight line to her execution. In America they have only the difference that they are carried on by the sturdy strain of parvenues, who can survive almost anything.

No, I am talking here about festivals in the country, which are celebrated solemnly or with childlike enjoyment.

The most important holiday of the year is Independence Day, July 4. That day we preferred to stay at home so that we heard the shooting and explosions only from a distance, and could watch the rockets rise above everything at night from our pasture hill.

Once it happened, as we learned first from our weekly paper, that the rockets did not arrive on time.

Two thousand people had come together in the town this day to see the parade, to marvel at the men, women, and children in old costumes dug out of trunks, to listen to the school band and to dance square dances — a kind of quadrille — in the streets.

But the fireworks were supposed to be the high point, and you can see how the man in charge of them must have been feeling the deepest mortification and keenest distress when he put the following explanation in the paper:

"On the 27th of June I had ordered the rockets. They were shipped on June 28th. But they didn't arrive until July 7th, three days after the holiday. I know that many came a long way to the celebration and were counting on seeing them, especially the children. I know how terrible the disappointment must have been, and I assure you that I was in despair. In any case, I want to thank you for making the rest of the celebration a success."

Another noisy holiday is Halloween, the night between October 31 and November 1, when the witches are abroad.

The word Halloween is supposed to be a combination of "the holy ones" and "even" and means "All Hallow's Eve" (the eve of All Saints' Day), although quite unholy things go on during this evening. Disguised figures growl and shriek in front of the houses, witches made of wax appear in the shop windows, skull lanterns are carried through the streets, and on All Saints' morning the farmers find their sleds on the roof, the harrow on the top of the chimney, the barn doors open . . . and editorials appear in the newspaper, saying that the mischief has again gone too far.

Three or four weeks later, on the last Thursday of the month of November, Thanksgiving is celebrated in memory of the first Thanksgiving, celebrated by the Pilgrim Fathers in 1623 after a terribly hard winter in their new colony. At that feast wild turkeys were eaten and in this way the turkey rose to the position of a ritual feast dish, something like the German Christmas goose or carp, or like lamb for Easter.

138

Every year Thanksgiving is formally proclaimed by the governor of Vermont and published in the *Vermont Standard*:

Whereas, since the days of our forefathers, who with great difficulty made a path through the wilderness to set up there the first colony to the glory of God and to enjoy freedom; and *whereas* it has become customary every year to set aside a time to give thanks to a gracious Providence for abundant blessings,

Inasmuch as we acknowledge the priceless privilege of freedom to live according to our own knowledge, conscience, and judgment, and affirm the responsibility this entails.

Therefore, as governor of Vermont, I declare the _____ day of November a day of Thanksgiving. Let us never forget that independence and responsibility are the characteristics of a strong nation. Let us fulfill our responsibilities to our fellow men at home and in the rest of the world. Remember that humanity the world over has the same concerns and the same needs, and think of the strength and the blessing which come from a united world. . . . Given and sealed with the seal of the state of Vermont on the 12th of November . . .

From the second winter on we were always invited to spend Thanksgiving with American friends.

This is perhaps the most American of all the holidays, and at the same time in the deepest sense a thanksgiving of the immigrants that they have escaped safely from their homeland and have survived life in the wilderness.

Many of the explorers and immigrants to America came for the purpose of seeking treasures — from gold to the elixir of eternal youth — that would make them rich and happy.

After King James I of England had announced, "I will make them conform, or I will hunt them from the land," nothing remained for those religious people who wished to worship in their own way but to flee first to Holland and later to journey to America.

Before they embarked to travel to an unknown land, finally and without thought of return, they held a day of prayer and penance, and for that their pastor chose a text from the book of Ezra (8:21): "Then I proclaimed a fast there at the river of Ahava, that we might afflict ourselves before our God, to seek

139

of him a right way for us, and for our little ones, and for all our substance."

No great-great-uncle of ours was there on that historic ship, the *Mayflower*, from whose small passenger list so many Americans descend that you get the impression after a while that it must have transported 500,000 ancestors.

We had no ancestors aboard that ship, but we had experienced our own "Mayflower," which we would never in our lives forget, when our ship left the still undestroyed city of Rotterdam, to bring us to an unknown land finally and without thought of return.

Now we celebrate Thanksgiving, and we sit with our friends around a table in their lovely old house with the high windows and spacious rooms.

The table is covered with a white cloth, and between the silver candelabra with light green, pleasant-smelling candles sits a great orange pumpkin, surrounded by rosy carrots, yellow and white onions, red beets, white and purple grapes, bright apples, and other tokens of the good harvest.

Outside it is frosty. The trees are bare, the grass in the meadows short and brown, waiting for a blanket of snow. Inside it is as warm as in those late fall days that they call Indian Summer.

On the table are fine porcelain, crystal glasses on silver coasters, and in glass dishes green olives, brown nuts, and pale celery. First there is a clam chowder that would do credit to a French chef. Then follows the turkey in dark brown splendor with a delicious stuffing. With it are small green peas, white onions in cream sauce, mashed potatoes, and the red cranberry sauce that has something of the taste of whortleberries.

The man and woman of the house sit at either end of the table. He carves the turkey. She hands him the plates, which she has filled with the vegetables. We sit at the sides of the table with the children, two little girls and a boy, enchanting creatures that look like pictures of former times.

Finally there is a pumpkin pie, whose pastry crust is tender and melting on the tongue.

Then there is still cheese, apples, and other fruit. After the meal we go into the blue living room to drink coffee around the fireplace and later to be served whiskey.

But even if it was not Thanksgiving, but another day when we were invited, it was festive, and the food was always prepared with elegant and delicious simplicity and was served by the man and woman of the house in the same manner.

In this house there were servants, sometimes two girls, sometimes one, once in a while none. But even that made no difference because she and he could cook as well as their best cook. Once we ate with them in the kitchen, and it was no less festive.

The house was a large farmhouse, situated on a hill, but when we drove up the steep driveway, we felt as if we were approaching a small castle.

I noticed her in the first year, while we were still summer visitors. I saw her often in the stores making purchases. In the second year we greeted each other. In the third I learned from a shopkeeper who she was, and was told that she had asked who I was.

From that came an acquaintance that developed into a friendship. Indeed, I don't know how we would have survived all our experiences without their help. They knew and could do absolutely everything.

He, who appeared like a well-dressed nobleman in the evening and wrote tender poetry, could be seen by day in undefinable, once-blue working clothes, driving a tractor on his wide acres, mowing or spreading manure. A friend helped him with the work, a hired man par excellence whose chief occupation was as a very gifted painter.

When I called the central switchboard, the operator knew that I probably wanted the number of that friend, my standard source for all questions from storing vegetables for the winter to recipes for pickling pork and smoking ham.

In 1944, when a hurricane from Florida was predicted, and we could not be sure that it would not go across Vermont as the unpredicted one did in the year 1938, I learned from her by telephone all the measures to take, where to shelter the animals and where to take refuge ourselves. She spoke very calmly and sensibly, and I thought then: she even knows how to deal with a hurricane.

She understood all house and farm work. She was a knowledgeable forester and decided herself which trees on their large forest holdings should be felled. She could not only direct others, but most of the work in her house she did with her own hands. At the same time she looked like a tall, slim aristocrat, and had nothing of the busy, perspiring, capable housewife about her.

This combination was new to us. We were accustomed in Europe to the idea that people from a certain class who busied themselves with spiritual matters should and must be spared the work of everyday living. But here were our friends, unique people, but not the only ones of this sort, who came from the best families and were blessed with money, but still worked with their hands and at the same time always found time to spend on higher things.

He had previously been a university professor, and combined a profound knowledge of literature, painting, history, and philosophy with a comprehensive knowledge of practical matters, so that abstract concepts came alive, and concrete things were lifted to a higher plane.

Of the other holidays, such as Columbus, Lincoln, and Memorial days, there is less to report. For us it was more or less a question whether and which stores would be closed, a decision which was often made at the last minute and could differ substantially in the different states, cities, and towns.

An important event in town life is Labor Day, which is celebrated on the first Monday in September and means that the summer vacation is over. After this day you may not wear summer clothing, shoes, and hats, no matter how hot it is.

For us farm people, the seasons and the weather play the main roles, and no one near us can stop reading, writing, and telling about them.

"Everyone talks about the weather, and no one does anything about it," Mark Twain is supposed to have said about New England weather. I believe that, if ever the most amazing apparatus against drought, hurricanes, and hail were discovered, you would still not know how to master *our* weather or how to shorten *our* winter.

It begins in November, around hunting season. Usually there is no snow, but it becomes cold, and a calm falls like that in the center of a typhoon.

142

The oppressive stillness is broken nine or ten days after its beginning by the thoroughly alarming hunting season.

There are great hunters, about whom the *Standard* reports:

"Among the mighty hunters of America we number Daniel Boone, Buffalo Bill, and more recently the Jenne brothers of Reading. They have taken three bucks and four bears and, when our reporter hurried to their farm to photograph them with their catch, two of the brothers were already back in the woods hunting bear. He found only the third brother, who was preparing to leave and impatient to join his brothers."

As much as we admire the great hunters, just so much are we annoyed by the lesser hunters. Any youth of fourteen can buy himself a hunting license for a little money and hurry into the woods with his father's gun. They shoot much, but very seldom hit a wild animal. They often hit themselves or each other, and they are apt to get lost. Zuck has had to show more than one such hunter the path back to civilization.

During the ten days of hunting season we have to dress up like trained monkeys, with red caps and bright-colored jackets, even if we just want to go through the woods to the corner to pick up the mail, so that they won't mistake us for fleeing deer.

At this time, too, unknown wild men sneak around the house. If one of them is cold and has become separated from his hunting party, he may come into the kitchen uninvited. There he sits by the stove, drinks from the whiskey flask he has brought with him, and now and then lifts the stove lid to spit his chewing tobacco onto the glowing coals.

At such times I always carried a kitchen knife around with me just in case, to feel more secure and to be able to defend myself against such unwished-for visitors.

My worst experience occurred, however, one time before hunting season, when no one was prepared for any trouble.

Zuck had gone away for two days. Since the beginning of our stay at the farm, two years and eight months earlier, he had not been away. But now he had to go to see his translator, who lived in the southern part of Vermont.

Winnetou and I were alone in the house for the first time. It was a time when we had no hired boy, and we felt abandoned and unprotected in the big, lonely house.

After taking care of the animals, we brought the dogs before dark into the garage, which could be reached from the kitchen door.

Winnetou and I crept together into my big double bed. She had taken the Civil War gun from the cellar, and I had placed a long, sharp bread knife on my night stand. We turned the light off early, but couldn't sleep and lay in the dark and waited.

We waited to see if anything would happen. We lay awake, ready to jump. We lay in wait for the danger. About one o'clock in the morning it happened.

From the forest road that was almost never traveled we heard a car coming.

We jumped out of bed and ran with weapon and knife into Zuck's room, through whose window we could see everything. We heard the motor howl as it fought its way along the road. Then the car stopped with a lurch by the pond.

The motor was turned off, and we heard men's muffled voices. Then it was quiet.

I opened the door of the room in which we were standing. Winnetou took her weapon in both hands like a club, and I unsheathed the bread knife.

Suddenly the woods were lighted as bright as day by a searchlight. We saw dark forms in the light, and then a terrible shooting from three guns began.

The dogs, who were penned up at the other end of the house and had gotten no wind of the strangers, began to bark like mad after the shooting.

We could now see quite clearly that there were three men. We heard them call and curse. We saw them carry something and load it onto the car. The motor was started up again, the searchlight turned off. They turned around by the pond, and the motor howled like a siren. It looked as if they would not be able to go back up the steep road into the woods. The wheels started to spin, and the gears ground.

"If they want to get tools from the garage and break in," Winnetou said through clenched teeth, "they will be torn to shreds by the dogs."

Suddenly the wheels caught, and the car struggled up the road and disappeared into the woods.

144

We stood and listened, but heard again only the soundlessness of the night.

"We have to go down and see if they are all gone," I said, shivering from the cold, although I was wearing a warm bathrobe.

"I think they must have shot the dogs," said Winnetou. "They aren't barking anymore."

We made our way into the kitchen, and then to the garage, where we found the dogs sleeping peacefully.

When Zuck returned, we looked like pale, careworn pioneer farm women who had just survived an Indian attack. We swore that the next time he went away we were going to go and spend the night in the village, or get a lumberjack to protect us.

Our fear was really justified because our visitors had been the worst kind of poachers, whose habit it is to blind wild animals with searchlights and then shoot down the blinded game.

This sort of poaching is severely punished, so you are dealing with unscrupulous trigger-happy characters who are ready to shoot more than game if they feel threatened.

Another time, when Zuck had to travel again, a friend of mine was visiting, a sturdy, courageous, valiant friend from Vienna. You could enjoy yourself with her, and in her presence I had no thought of fear. But in spite of her merry temperament she suffered from insomnia, so on the third night that we were alone as a household of women she took a good dose of sleeping medicine. Therefore she missed it entirely when around two o'clock in the morning our entire house seemed to be surrounded by wandering lights that danced on the hill, leapt in the trees, and crept through the meadow.

This ghostly drama was interrupted from time to time by shots, but there was something so uncanny about it that Winnetou and I had the feeling that this time we were not dealing with natural and normal things, but perhaps also not with bad and wicked ones.

So we shut the deep sleeper in her room, barred the door of my bedroom, put the weapon between us in the bed, and went back to sleep. When we called someone in the village the next day, we learned that there had been a racoon hunt in our vicinity. These animals are hunted with many flashlights, searched for in the trees, and shot down.

That was hunting season, which we had to watch without ammunition or weapons, since as foreigners we were not permitted to have firearms.

By the beginning of hunting season the house and barn were ready for winter. Outside, as protection from the snow, they were wrapped in strong brown paper to the height of the windows and looked like half-wrapped packages being prepared for shipment.

Then in front of every window was hung a double window, appropriately called a storm window.

The barn walls and a few exposed parts of the wall of the house were first wrapped with a batt-like material and then covered with slabs, while all water pipes were put into white coverings, a porous mass that looked like a plaster cast so that the rooms through which the pipes ran looked like Red Cross stations for first aid.

These labors against the frost we had to do every year ourselves. I hated the insulation, which was made of a demonic material that stuck through the work gloves and liked to sift down inside our clothes around our backs and chests, so that we would think we were wearing hair shirts. But when the house had been readied in this fashion, we could look ahead to winter patiently and in good spirits. We watched the snow fall and pile up, felt the arctic cold of January and February, and heard with amazement on the radio that Moscow was only thirty degrees below zero at a time when we had fallen to forty-five degrees below zero.

Then came the first news item like this:

"Rupert Morton states that he has seen a blackbird, and Leslie Sawyer thinks she heard a frog croak. . ."

Or:

"It has been reported that a few hardy souls and optimists have fought their way through the snow to the maple trees, have begun to tap the trees already, and believe that the maple sap will soon run into the pails."

This announcement means that soon bright sunny days will follow frosty nights, the maple sap will drip into the metal pails, the smoke stacks of the sugar houses in the woods will smoke day and night, and we will sit in the kitchen until two or three in the morning and watch the sap boil down.

146

Then at the end of March comes this brief note:

"The snow that fell from the 2nd of November to the 16th of March amounted to fifteen feet altogether. The spring thaw has set in suddenly and fills this reporter with the hope that snow and cold are disappearing."

The thaw lasts only three days. Then comes sleet, and we creep on all fours over glare ice to the barns, and Zuck spends his days spreading ashes on all the paths. The animals' drinking water has to be changed every three hours, because it freezes in the drinking troughs, and we freeze with it to the marrow of our bones. Even the news, "On Eastern morning Mrs. Harold Stillwell found a snowdrop blooming in her garden and saw on the same day a great group of wild geese flying northward . . . ," cannot raise our spirits because we have to read this good news in the dark. At this time the windows of our first floor rooms are still covered with snow, some entirely, some four fifths, some a third, depending on location. It gives us the feeling that we have been covered by an avalanche. That is the time when the telephone, if it is not out of order, is kept constantly in use.

We complain over all the nine lines, and we give voice to our impatience and despair. We can't bear to look at the snow anymore. We are sure that it will never stop snowing again, and we no longer believe that spring can ever come.

In the course of these comforting conversations we slide suddenly without noticing into "mud season." That is the beginning of spring, when everywhere the ice breaks up suddenly, and the roads become impassable swamps.

Then every year it becomes obvious overnight how small the number of paved highways is in the country, and how long the roads are that lead to them.

Now life and motion come to our village. The tow trucks from the garage are constantly called out to rescue cars that have sunk into the mud. You telephone home: "I am just leaving town now. If I'm not there in an hour, don't worry. I'll be stuck in the mud."

The cars move like turtles and lizards through the swamp. At many places the mud looks like bubbling lava, and then there are ruts in which the wheels stick fast as though in sinkholes. In other places running brooks flow across the road.

Then the brown-black swamp appears again. Yet the wet dirt, which splashes over the roof of the car, smells like spring.

You arrive home shaking all over from the effort that it takes to steer the wheels against the mud. You rail at the impossible, miserable state of the roads. You demand that finally a concrete road should be built between the sizable villages, a road from which the snow water would simply roll off, and which would make the traffic independent of the weather.

You tell of the colorful curses of the travelers you have met, and of the immense difficulty of pulling them out. Then you run to the telephone to hear how the others are doing, and at the same time get news about which spots in the roads are the very worst.

But through all these excited conversations rings the joy that we have once more survived the ice and the snowdrifts, and that we can now get out into the mud.

Spring is short, and soon summer comes, and with it the animals from the woods.

That is the time when one must empty the garbage can carefully because a skunk might be sitting in it. The skunk is a beautiful and friendly animal, but when it is frightened or disturbed it uses its scent glands. In just a few minutes the entire house is enveloped in a gas cloud whose stench is greater than that of a stink bomb.

Then the woodchuck emerges. He is a kind of large marmot, harmless to people but causing great damage in the fields.

In the early spring he is the "groundhog" of legend, who predicts the duration of winter. If he comes out on a specific day in early spring and sees his own shadow, he goes back in and has six more weeks of hibernation. However, if there is hazy, dreary weather on that day, his shadow cannot frighten him — he has slept out, and spring will come soon.

One evening we heard a panting and rattling, as though someone were trying to sweep off wood with a steel broom. Zuck went out to the double toilet in the shed — every old farmhouse has one — and turned the beam of his pocket flashlight on one of the seats. It revealed a porcupine, who was poking its head up through the opening and rubbing its neck comfortably around the rim. From then on we avoided the two-seater in the evening.

148

Then came the time when Zuck came home beaming and told how he had met a mother bear with cubs in the woods. She had stood up on her hind legs and growled angrily, and he had had trouble keeping the dogs on their leashes.

In the same week I found in the *Standard* the amazing story of Bear 1902, Bear 1944:

"Mrs. and Mrs. Lamontaine are astonished about the bear coincidence. When they were married in 1902, they went on their wedding trip through the woods with horse and wagon, and there stood a bear in the middle of the road in front of them. Last Thursday they drove through the woods by car on their 42nd anniversary. There was a bear standing in the middle of the road in front of them."

The panther stories, however, seemed much more serious to me, though we were constantly assured that panthers had long since died out here in the East.

In the woods about ten minutes from our house is a large light-colored granite boulder quite near the path. Under it, they say, a huge treasure of gold is hidden.

Once I saw a powerful wildcat sitting on the rock in broad daylight. It spat, as though it had to defend the enchanted guardian of the treasure. On that same cliff a lynx was crouching one evening as Zuck came up the path. It gave that shrill, moaning cry that fills the brave with fear, the unsuspecting with horror, and makes the timid shudder.

Whenever I went by this rock, I thought about the panthers that used to spring from the trees onto the backs of unsuspecting passersby, knocking them down and killing them.

In America nothing is very long ago. The last Indian raid in our area took place in 1793, and the last panther was reported in 1883.

Now appears this item:

"The panther again. Mr. and Mrs. Ralph Stevens do not want to state outright that they have seen a panther, but they say that they have seen a wild animal quite near their house. They say that it has a long tail like a dog, but short legs and a cat head."

Now we go quickly to high summer. There are often hot days, but the nights are almost always cool.

This is the time of guests.

They pour in and stay for shorter or longer times. Some-

149

times they are only here for an evening.

Once we had paying guests all summer. Since that time I have wished I could own a guest house. But I would like to have help with the dishwashing.

In late summer the great butchering took place, a sad and ugly occasion, when it was a comfort and joy to have the house crowded with guests. After the pigs were killed came the great feast, where we supplied the sausages, and the guests the drinks.

The kitchen was overrun with people.

There stood a surgeon friend with Zuck at the sink cleaning up pig intestines. An artist stuffed sausages with me. A university professor ran liver and milt through a meat grinder, a publisher washed dishes on an assembly line. Michi prepared boiled dumplings with a friend from Vienna. Winnetou sorted the drinks people had brought, while a group of guests who were tired from the work made themselves cocktails in the cool cellar with telling results and called up to the kitchen that we should let the work be and enjoy life with them.

This celebration went happily through all its phases and ended in happiness and harmony just before the time for the morning milking.

On another day, when no party was planned, but twenty-four chickens had to be slaughtered, plucked, and cleaned by four o'clock in the afternoon to be taken to the freeze locker in town, the translator-author from southern Vermont arrived like a gift from heaven with his wife.

The men had to withdraw for serious conversation, while I stood with the translator's wife in the kitchen in front of a mountain of plucked chickens. I really didn't know how I could carry on an intellectual conversation while cleaning chickens. She was an intelligent, educated person, but I didn't know how familiar she was with country life. But since she was a young American woman of the old school, she rolled up her sleeves, demanded an apron, and soon we stood together at the big table and picked out one chicken after another.

When I had to spend three days after the pig slaughtering cutting up lard, rendering fat, smelling cracklings, and cooking soup, I protested with the Old Testament injunction that I could not see or touch pork for months — shortening the time from the original prohibition because I am particularly fond of pork.

After plucking and cleaning the chickens — Zuck did the actual slaughtering — I was sure that the horror of it would linger all year.

But this time it was different. The job itself and the smell were unchanged, but the time flew by with lively conversation. By the eighth chicken we had discussed the effects of bad pedagogy. By the twelfth chicken we were arguing the delicate question of theater and translation. Up to the sixteenth chicken we explored literature in general. It took only two chickens to describe the place of man in Europe, and with the remaining six we were scarcely able to establish the significance of woman in America.

By exactly quarter past three the chickens were packed cleanly in my car, and I could deliver them on time to the deep freezer man in town.

That same evening we marvelled in speechless wonder over our guest. He not only had a command of eight languages, but could also perform magic tricks on a scale far beyond home entertainment at the level of a professional artist.

When it turned out that he had worked as a magician at one time, I gave up trying to classify people from that time on, or to place them in any kind of system.

There are elegant, quiet old men who were once whalers, powerful lumberjacks who were tired of being lawyers, salesmen who have taught school for years, long-time housewives who have explored half the world on dangerous expeditions. Men who are the most amusing and worldly company turn out to be parsons. This means that you can find out in just a little time what kind of person you are dealing with, but his work and position seem to have played no decisive role and left no impression on him. His calling hasn't poured him into a mold whose shape he has taken. This striking lack of structure bothered us at first. We were puzzled and amazed until we realized that here was a new pattern with new rules.

In the fall the guests left, and flocks of birds on their flight south often set down on our pond.

Fall appeared in advertisements:

"Does anyone need Green Mountain potatoes? We have

them. Come and get them."

"We have a cider press. Come and bring your apples with or without worms. We will press them out for you to the last drop."

And here is a man who hasn't found himself a place for the winter:

"Artist who understands farm work seeks a farm for the winter to buy or lease, condition not important."

The October days come, startling in their blazing color, warm and unsettling like spring. The wood is stored in the shed. Smoke rises straight up from the chimneys. The house is made snug. The bears go into hibernation. A good solitude and a winged peace enfold the house.

Drude

When I tell about the land and the people, the animals and the farm, I cannot keep quiet about a creature that lived in our house, hidden, invisible, only appearing occasionally.

It is not that it particularly wanted to be with us or to live in our house.

It is everywhere, in all houses, in all lands, in all parts of the world. We give it a hundred names and explain it a thousand ways.

In folklore it is a real being and closely related to the evil spirits the Germans call Alp or Mahr that slip through the key-hole at night and sit on a sleeper's chest, choke him, steal his breath, and hold him captive in terrible dreams.

An Alp can appear as a spirit, or he can come from far away over the water, like the "Mahr from England." But he can also be sent out by people who have an Alp in themselves and "send the Alp to others by their thoughts when they are filled with anger or hatred."

The Alp goes out from the eyebrows of these "Alp-carriers," as they are called, "like a little white butterfly, and sits down on the chest of the sleeper to whom he is sent."

But I want to tell about Drude, the sister of Alp and Mahr, and to try to personify in her the depressing waking dream and the condition that comes from the weather, especially from humid winds and the lack of ultraviolet rays of the sun, from an overfilled stomach, poor nutrition, or psychic disturbances, and which can be the forerunner of depression, melancholy, and dejection.

153

In America they call her the "Blues," as if Drude and the Alp dressed up in night hues.

She is known everywhere, but especially on isolated farms. She has many shapes. To one person she appears as fog, to another as cobwebs. She can be a heavy stone or a dark cloud, an animal, seaweed, or an invisible, empty nothing. But however she appears, she has the characteristic that she is anxious about minor misfortunes, worries about petty difficulties, is burdened by small annoyances. She never permits an honest passion like pain or grief to appear. Her pendulum swings between gnawing dissatisfaction and suffocating anxiety. She soaks up secret cares and mixes trouble and worry to an unrecognizable mass of dust, whose gray particles eat into the cracks of daily life.

She appears at night and often follows you into the daylight.

You wake up at night, and the whole dark room is filled with calamity and misfortune.

You try to close your eyes, but eyelids are no protection against the burning darkness. Your head seems to be a magnet, and the thoughts, which have scattered in all directions, turn into fantastic creatures and confused images as soon as they enter its field.

You hear the apocalyptic riders. You see a procession of people that you recognize as individuals and as a group, but you don't know who belongs to the living and who is already dead. You are far away and free, and at the same time trapped on a small island.

You know you are no longer a foreigner, but have put down roots. You love the house, but in those nights you hate the work that is connected with it. The dust creeps back like the spiders in the rafters, to appear again and again. The piles of dishes lie like coral reefs where you could be shipwrecked. The mending basket grows like dough that has too much yeast in it. The stalls, the sheds, the workshop, the repairs—you will never find time to take care of them all!

The expression "time lies heavy on my hands" takes on new meaning.

It lies heavy on your feet, too. It is as if you were walking on the face of a great clock, in circles without beginning or end, and the clock hands describe the path, but no longer tell the

154

time. Six, nine, twelve, three become road signs that you pass as you do the same thing over and over again, no longer aware that they refer to time. For time is probably the most incomprehensible of all measurements, and there can be days, weeks, and months when you feel as if you had lost all feeling, hearing, and vision of time.

Everything that you do seems to have no more sense or goal. All that remains is worry about the future. The cold of winter makes such nights worse. It comes into the house through the walls and goes across your face as if you had come too close to an open fireplace.

Never before had I experienced cold in such a visible, tangible form, never before realized how closely biting cold is related to scorching heat.

I tried to think back to something definite, for as soon as you give a memory a solid form or think something through, Drude has to retire to a corner to wait there for another wave of disorder and confusion.

I thought of the ten-year-old peasant boy whom I had taken to Salzburg with me once to treat to ice cream.

He had never in his life before tasted it, and when he shoved a tremendous piece of chocolate ice cream into his mouth, he roared, spit it out in a wide arc, shook his arms and balled his fists as if he had been showered with ice water, and shouted with his mouth wide open, as if he had swallowed glowing coals, "hot, hot, hot, hot. . . !" This cold, smoldering, glowing, scorching cold we had come to know well in Vermont.

It was a season of unendurable cold, more than we could deal with, and the wind's whistling and howling made our eardrums hurt. Winter, the incubation period of Drude.

When I got mired in a cloudbank of melancholy thoughts, help sometimes appeared.

On the stroke of three at night, the door of the iron stove that stood in the upstairs hall and had to heat all the rooms was opened with a rattle. It had a mighty frame and needed nourishment every three hours. I heard the heavy logs being laid in one by one and the closing of the iron door. Then a soft crackling began, like machine gun fire. In between, there were explosions like the landing of heavy mortars. Then it turned into an irregular clicking. All these sounds showed the heating of the stove itself at the stage before it was warmed up and could itself radiate heat.

It made me think of heat as one of the great Egyptian plagues in our winter life.

During six months of the year Zuck had to put wood into the iron stove on the stroke of three at night, walking in his sleep, without waking up, and yet robbed of his best rest by the demon of necessity.

That was our heat. I think we would all have frozen to death if Zuck had not been such a fanatic fire-tender. But it was not so much a matter of our well-being. The main thing was the water system that must be kept from freezing. We could no longer worry about whether we were cold or warm. We always had other things to think about.

We took care of the pipes like babies, the animals like children, and the stoves like temperamental animals. Wood was sacred.

We stood at the center of everything, and to survive we had to be watchman, caretaker, and protector, constantly blocking a return to chaos.

For Zuck wood and heating were totem, taboo, and fetish at the same time. So I called him a pyromanticist, a combination of pyromaniac and romanticist.

When I watched how he piled the kindling crossways in the big open fireplaces, laid the split logs like a grating over them, and crowned his building with a mighty log of yellow birch, when I saw how he set fire to the structure on the corners and ends and the flames shot high, I saw his work connected to secret magic formulas and charms from the primeval forest. When he put the gigantic logs into the iron stoves, when he set and arranged them, then I realized how fire was once thought to be a gift from heaven to men and must be treated reverently.

Finally there was still the kitchen stove, which needed to be filled with coal morning and evening, and had to be shaken morning and evening with a deafening noise to make its ashes drop down into the pit, making a smell like a rusty locomotive on a local run. When Zuck threw the new coal onto the glowing fire with a swing of the black hod, he reminded me of the fireman on a ship, who had to bring the boiler to the point of exploding to escape the pursuit of enemy cruisers.

156

It was only the hands of the pyromanticist that did not look like those of a fireman.

It was part of the Drude and Alp nights that you felt of your own scratched hands again and again and rubbed your broken fingernails. You longed for calluses and thick skin as a protective covering against sensitivity, but felt that your misshapen hard hands were foreign elements on your own body.

Even though we worked much of the time with gloves, as is customary in America—and there are gloves of all types, from heavy leather to fabric to soft rubber—our fingernails were still scarred with cuts, and calluses were beginning to make a painful appearance near our fingertips.

For Zuck, however, working with wood and heating began to break the skin at the base of his nails. His palms and fingers were scarred and scratched by splinters that could not always be removed. Drops of blood settled into the cracks and scratches and hardened quickly to scabs when they were dried by the heat of the fire.

The keys of his typewriter, the a, e, r, and other much-used letters, showed brownish spots, and it was sometimes simply bloody fingers that kept him from giving his penciled notes form and shape with the typewriter, even when there was suddenly and unexpectedly time to write.

Since you get used to thinking of the things you work with as having a life of their own, Zuck's anger was not usually directed at himself or at his existence, but at the typewriter. He beat the table with his injured hands and shouted that he wanted to take care of this machine, this . . .

Then followed a stream of colorful, creative curses, from which we could gather that he had decided to smash the machine once and for all, to beat the stove to pieces, to stamp out the fires and scatter the ashes to the winds.

That was the moment when something definite had to be done to counteract this clear expression of destruction. Two solutions were available with two different properties. You dipped your hands in one to wash and soften them. The other solution, reddish or deep blue in color, you brushed onto the wounded places to heal and harden them.

For one or two days after such treatment Zuck could write again and hammer away on his typewriter, provided that there

157

was no storm, no smoking stove, no sick animal, no leaky roof, and that no accident or misfortune occurred, things we had come to regard as normal parts of life.

When worries about cold, heating, and hands like beds of nettles had subsided, the thought of the typewriter was the worst, a nightmare by itself. Sometimes it seemed as if I saw it as a personification of Drude, lying in wait on the desk in Zuck's room.

The rattling of the machine was like the motion and sound of a measuring instrument, a seismograph that indicates and records.

Sometimes it sounded like the quick, regular hammering of a mill, at others like the rolling of great boulders in an avalanche. Sometimes it was like the slow dripping of water from a wet cliff, or like the tapping of the cane of a blind man seeking his way. Or it stopped, and it was quiet for days, weeks, and months.

We had become accustomed with time not to speak of Zuck's work, the way you never mention an incurable illness, or push a dangerous illness away from you by not mentioning it.

In the first year on the farm he still had plans and illusions. The plans extended like rays in many directions, but carrying them out was interrupted, the way a radius is limited and cut off by too narrow a circumference. The themes wouldn't fit together. The transitions didn't succeed. The way from first inspiration to production was interrupted.

Yes, the whole complex which had to do with free-lance work could be compared to a bush, packed for shipping with well-wrapped, balled roots, and tied branches, and set in a dark corner of the barn to be planted on a cool evening.

As for the illusions, he shared those with many others.

In one of the unbearable nights I tried to drive Drude away with reading. This is a rewarding undertaking when you succeed in mixing the sublime with the ordinary in the proper dosage. This time I found an article in a magazine with the title, "Farming Isn't Fun," an attack on farming which I read with relief and enjoyment, because it makes you happy when someone else expresses in writing what you have thought silently and angrily to yourself.

This American fellow sufferer wrote:

158

I began to farm my acres in Vermont in the free time allowed by my work as a writer. Now I have come to the point where I write in the little free time I can steal from the farm work. If it never rained, I would never get to my typewriter at all, because the corn and potatoes need my attention. My friends who are tied to their typewriters look at my farmyard, my barns, and my fields with longing. They long to dig in Mother Earth. They speak of the fresh and happy work with ax and spade. I envy them just as much. In three years I have had enough and have become tired of farm work. I am, furthermore, just terribly tired. . . . Haying certainly makes a pretty picture when you sit in a shady corner on the edge of the field and watch the happy countryman at work. Prose and verse have sung and celebrated this torment as a pleasant recreation, probably because none of those writers have ever swung a hay fork for hours in a sun-scorched field. But I have. I know how it feels when sweat drips out of all pores — my skin feels like that of an eel, and I am on the edge of total dehydration in spite of all the liquid I have thrown down my throat. It is strange that even Vermonters get romantic when the maple syrup time comes, and they celebrate the time with parties. . . . For me it means nothing but slaving with forty-pound cans of sap. My arms get stretched to ape-like length. Bushes, stones, and hidden sticks bruise my legs. Twigs whip my unprotected face, and my lungs, legs, and shoulders hurt almost as much as my arms. . . . It is supposed to be pleasant to come back to the comfortable house after a healthy day's work in field and wood. That's the way it is described by those who write about amateur farming, and also by those who write novels. They forget that, before he can sit down, the returning farmer has to do the dirtiest work of all, the barn work. They forget that he has to serve his animals as masseur, waiter, chamber maid, and garbage man. . .

At this point I started to laugh. On the one hand, reading about the same anger, the same annoyance you have felt always stirs sympathetic laughter. On the other, it was unmistakable how Drude had tripped up this farm writer and now held him in her claws.

Nothing annoys or angers Drude more than laughter. It

works as if you dusted her with DDT and fed her rat poison.

You are lucky when you can drive her away with laughter, but it is not something you can count on, just as you can't count on any lessening of the load of work.

Drude, Alp, Mahr, Blues — all are nothing more and nothing less than the fear that you won't be able to carry the load, which is made up of many components and is unchangeable.

It seems to work like a balance. On one of the scales lie the threatening real facts, and in the other must be placed that irrational but dependable strength that keeps the balance through thick and thin.

It is this strength that interests the blues, that they try to attack and destroy from all sides.

There are many ways to escape them, though they are ancient, sly, and evil in nature.

You can run away from them and become a moving target. You can withdraw to the mountain top and meditate. You can try to draw a balance by calculating debits and credits and come out in the black. You can compare your lot with that of others. In our time, we are able to visualize at any moment the fate of millions in all its hardness and cruelty, and this makes you thankful that you have come away with only a black eye.

There are many other escape routes and weapons against Alp and Drude, but you must not underestimate the strength of these enemies, even though at first they only produce feelings like ill humor, disgust, discomfort, indifference, and discouragement.

They sit in the background and wait for you to attribute false explanations for the circumstances that produce them, for you to try to blame others for your own mistakes. They wait for you to mix cause and effect and bring confusion and disorder into the simplest things. They poison your pleasure and feed the flames of anxiety. They want to prove to you that you are lying on a bed of nails in a state of trance like an Indian fakir, and if you are awakened you can be torn by every nail.

They should be watched as they crouch on the threshold, for admitted they can lead to sickness, insanity, and suicide. They have been a plague in all lands, to all peoples, in all times. Procopius, a Greek historian of the time of the migrations, described them fourteen hundred years ago in an account of the land and people of the island Thule:

160

On this island something very strange happens every year. For at the time of the summer solstice the sun does not set for forty days, and at the time of the winter solstice the sun does not rise for forty days, and the island is wrapped in eternal night. Melancholy attacks the people because they cannot see each other at this time. . . . But when thirty-five days of this long night have passed, a few people are sent up to a mountain peak, and as soon as they see a trace of sun they notify those waiting below, and call to them that the sun will shine in five days. Then they celebrate a great festival in the darkness. That is the great celebration of the people, and I can imagine that, even though the same thing happens year after year, the people of Thule are always attacked by the fear that the sun might stay away forever.

The people of Thule were hunted into melancholy by the blue spirits, frightened by the constellations, and threatened by the end of the world.

After fourteen hundred years we have progressed so far that the end of the world will perhaps be technically possible in a not too distant time.

Doubtless there has never before been a time like our atomic age, when the concepts of maintaining or destroying life, the choice between "Energy" and "Bomb," have been so clear and have become a part of common speech and daily life without a detour through philosophy and creed.

We are all in one boat — the experimental animals, the goats and pigs, are there with us — and the test on Bikini affects us all.

But there is still the "Energy," the storehouse or reservoir of those powers which men, animals, and other creatures possess as long as they live and want to continue living.

In the old legends there is a charm against Drude: "Drude, Drude, come tomorrow, I can wait to borrow sorrow." This forces her to run away and to reappear the next day in the form of a person coming to borrow something.

That means that she has become weak, a suppliant, a debtor, a poor enemy. You must treat her with kindness and caution to keep the strength you need to overcome her.

For you will always have to live with Drude and will have to get the better of her again and again.

161

The Way to the Library

Through the Great Migrations I came to the library. I had gotten my hands on the writings of Paulus Diakonos and Procopius, who lived at the end and in the middle of that period. I could not pull myself away from that dark age thereafter, and I kept wanting to learn more about it.

Not from historians who wrote eleven to nineteen centuries later, but through the eyewitnesses themselves, who had lived with and experienced the Great Migrations. For example, Gregory of Tours, who wrote in the wild times of the Merovingians, or Procopius, who advised and flattered the Byzantine Emperor Justinian and at the same time hated him deeply; Paulus, who lived as hostage and friend at the court of Charlemagne; Benedict, who opposed chaos with an order that extended from common sense and knowledge of men to creative wisdom; and Gregory the Great, monk, saint, poet, administrator, pope, general, Roman, diplomat, preacher, and expert on all human weaknesses. The horrors of that time are no longer able to shock us — they were far less calculated and intentional than the tortures used in our own day.

My preoccupation with the early Middle Ages, the childhood history of the people whose dark traits are mirrored in a sick revival in our adult, conscious age, was in equal parts strange and familiar. Because of this it was not surprising that the library in which I could find all the material about it in Latin, English, and German seemed to me a place of enchanted unreality, an island, a promised land.

It was also not to be wondered at that the way to it was long and difficult, consisted of many stages, and that I had to pay ransom, so to speak, both coming and going, to buy myself free from daily living, to earn the right to be allowed to set foot on the island. It was obvious that preparations for such a significant journey must be made as carefully as possible, and that they had to be started at least twenty-four hours in advance.

It was not only that the library was a long way from our house.

In summer the trip by car took exactly fifty-five minutes from the kitchen door at the farm to the entrance of the library. In the winter this simple commuting trip became an expedition, and if I closed the kitchen door behind me at seven in the morning, I rarely stood at the library entrance before noon.

In the summer I could manage to go once a week; in the winter it depended on the weather.

In the summer I rarely remained overnight in the university town in whose center the library stood; I was accustomed to start for home about 10:30, after the usual closing time of the library.

In the winter I stayed one to two nights in town and had a place there with good friends.

There are libraries everywhere in America. Each little community, each village has its own library in its own little building.

These village libraries are mostly open twice a week in the evening. The children go there and the people of the village take out books and bring books back. These little collections often have a considerable number of works from early American history through Dickens to the most recent American literature. There are books about agriculture, about the history of the community, detective stories, and above all children's books.

The towns have larger libraries. Our neighboring town has, for example, a very imposing library which contains in addition to books a lovely collection of Chinese porcelain.

163

The cities have impressive libraries of massive dimensions. The reading rooms of the public library in New York hold five hundred people.

The largest library of all in America is the Library of Congress in Washington. They say that it possesses all the books of the world.

Most of these libraries were founded by donors and are maintained by donations.

But the university libraries are something quite unique. I had the good fortune to come upon the Dartmouth College library, an experience with the fateful quality of making me sure that I could never be happy anywhere else.

Once I had settled in there, all other libraries, especially those in Europe, seemed like just cafeterias, railroad waiting rooms, tax offices, or museums. Their varying and uncertain hours, their many prohibitions, their attendants in gray smocks all made me feel like a petitioner, or a scholarship student who cannot afford to buy the important books and must therefore depend on charity and who has to be watched so that he doesn't walk off with anything.

But most of all what disturbs me in the European libraries is the dullness, the stolidness that the reading rooms exude from their dusty pores that makes you drag home like a snail with the book they have let you borrow.

In my library you are a guest. The attendants are dressed as if for a tea party which they will hold in the rooms of the library. Your hosts pride themselves on having or being able to order the books in which you are interested.

It is all hospitable and unforced. The building, the rooms, the way the building is divided, and the people there all contribute to an atmosphere of meaning and importance. The meaning is in the books, stored up as latent energy, and the important thing is to carry this energy over into life and make it useful to living people.

This is my library, and it means nothing less to me than landing on another planet.

When I step into the first section of the revolving door that leads into the entrance hall of the library, I sense that all my oppressive ghosts and evil spirits have turned into blue smoke behind me and have dispersed like mist.

164

The preparations for the trip consisted in cooking ahead, telephoning, and doing and noting everything on the "frightful" lists.

The cooking would be large quantities of things like baked beans with salt pork, an American national dish known as Boston baked beans, which is cooked in an earthen pot in the oven for twelve hours. Or it was a Szegedine goulash, or lentils with ham, or mutton with cabbage, in short, a meal that would only improve with reheating so that Zuck lived securely and comfortably for two or three days on reheated meals.

Since he could also cook quite well himself, he brought variety to these solid one-dish meals with additions of grilled meat, omelets, scrambled eggs, etc., and lived during these days like a man in a hunting shack, demonstrating that he can get along without female help.

In America intellectual worth and manly strength are not proved by avoiding the work of everyday living. It is thought neither honorable nor lovable for a man to behave like a helpless child. On the other hand, it is not regarded as a sign of slavery and unhappy domination by women when American men are able to do every kind of housework and sometimes even know something about the care of infants.

In this independence of the men lies a danger for the women. Since the men no longer need to be taken care of and waited on by women, a marriage can scarcely be founded on the popular idea that a man will never want to leave his wife because in the course of time she becomes his indispensable nursemaid and customary cook.

We came to an agreement about housework that represented a mixture of the European and the American.

On my return from the library, I found the kitchen and house in perfect order, the dishes washed, the floors swept, everything picked up. I could throw myself with renewed strength and fresh spirit into the housework, from which Zuck was once again freed.

After cooking ahead came a thorough checking of the lists. I dared not forget anything, especially in the time of gasoline rationing when the gas would cover only one trip a week to the nearest town and one trip every three weeks to the nearest university town.

Over the kitchen table, along the wall like a fresco, ran a list on which was written down everything that we needed for the kitchen. On the door to the garage hung the list of all the feeds. On another door was fastened a slip of paper on which needed repairs were noted.

On it were: check roof; kitchen door squeaks; ball in the toilet is broken; geese's water trough leaks; kitchen table leg is loose.

These notes in no way meant that a handyman should be called to fix these things, but only that we needed to get the materials to repair them ourselves.

Besides these orderly lists that looked down on us with stern injunctions like the tablets of the law from all the walls, there was a blackboard on which current wishes and demands of individual family members were written, in colored chalk, in disconnected, irregular fashion.

When the children were home, the blackboard was especially confused.

For example, there stood in Michi's handwriting (and she loved to write her wishes on the board with yellow chalk): nail polish, chocolate, Rilke's poems, vanilla, blue wool, cinnamon sticks, stockings.

Winnetou used blue chalk for: corn feed for the chicks, castor oil for the cats, Mozart's sonatas for piano, cigarettes, beef steaks.

Zuck's list, in white chalk, looked something like this: typewriter ribbon, a heart for the dogs, liver for the cats, adhesive tape, tobacco, Grimm's Legal Antiquities, look up material on Paul Bunyan and Johnny Appleseed, don't forget Barbara Blomberg, whiskey, shoulder of lamb, knife sharpener, rat poison.

My list was uninteresting and ran like this: pack up six dozen eggs, something to prevent clogged drains, onion salt, tuna, beer, wine, peppercorns, etc. This monotony was because I made a special list for the books I wanted to borrow from the library, and so never mixed the Saints of the Merovingians with paprika, or set Charlemagne next to bay leaves, and never had the Germanic kings following soap powder. Everything on those lists had to be copied carefully onto notepaper and organized by the three or four different towns in

166

which I could find the separate articles.

Then I packed the eggs in special aluminum crates that were divided into layers of cartons. In each individual section was placed an egg wrapped in paper, because this kind of packing protected the egg during transportation, even if bounced around wildly.

Often I also took slaughtered chickens, ducks, or geese with me to sell.

But the heaviest part of the load I carried was the books that I was bringing back to the library. They usually numbered at least a full dozen.

After packing up and copying lists, I did an extra thorough cleaning of the house, to leave it in good condition for Zuck. Finally I went to the barn, checked the animals, and told them to behave themselves and not to get a disease of any sort while I was away.

After all these intensive preparations, there was still the most important matter — the telephone conversation with Harry. Everything depended on this conversation, because on it I based my decision whether or not to use my own car. I called Harry in the evening.

Harry knows everything, can do everything, understands everything.

He milks his cows at 6:00 in the morning and feeds his pigs. At 7:15 he collects the mail and drives the school bus to the next town. At 8:30 he is a salesman in a meat store. At 3:30 in the afternoon he brings the mail and the school children back from town to the village. At 6:00 he milks his cows and feeds his pigs. He is a farmer, postman, and salesman, but above all he understands and loves cars, and they flourish under his care.

Often in winter, when I went off the road into the ditch in deep snow and couldn't get my car back onto the icy pavement again, I stopped a motorist and asked him to tell Harry that I was sitting in the ditch at one of the four places where you could expect to slide into the ditch in winter.

Then Harry came to the indicated spot, pleasant, untroubled, cheerful, and it seemed to me as though my car pricked up its ears and nickered softly at the sight of him.

Then Harry sat down behind the steering wheel, and the car jumped out of the ditch, panting and trembling in its flanks, and slid and danced on the icy road until Harry brought it into strict control. Then it ran as though it had never been in the ditch.

That is Harry, the auto trainer. We left the car with him in the winter. He protected and cared for it, and every morning he let it run so that the motor wouldn't freeze. That is Harry, whom I had to call on the evening before my expedition to ask him how my car was doing and whether he believed it would be happy to run the next morning. He couldn't be sure, Harry would answer. It still started this morning, but the temperature was beginning to drop, and it would probably be a cold night. (Whenever I wanted to go to the library, the temperature always sank far below zero, or it climbed for a snowstorm.)

Each time he told me to call him again early in the morning, and then we would see.

In the nights before these trips I was restless, getting up to look at the thermometer, or opening the window to sniff and see whether a snowstorm was on the way.

At 5:30 the alarm clock rang, and I got up. It was pitch black, but Zuck had already built roaring fires in all the stoves, and it was warm in the house.

We ate breakfast half asleep in the warm kitchen.

At 6:30 I called up Harry.

"Will it start?" I asked.

"Not yet," answered Harry, "but maybe soon."

"Call me when it's running," I told Harry.

"All right," said Harry.

After a quarter of an hour our ring sounded.

"It's running," said Harry.

That was the clear, simple sentence for which I had been waiting, restless but resigned.

The answer, "It won't start," meant that I had to take the school bus to the next town to wait there for an hour for a bus that would go over the snow-covered mountains but was usually late and brought me only to the nearest town that had a railway station. There I had to wait two hours for another bus that would take me in less than a quarter hour to the university town.

In short, the trip without my own car meant waiting and carrying heavy packages. That took a quantity of patience and

168

meekness which I could not always bring forth cheerfully.

I can well remember one certain winter morning.

At seven o'clock sharp I left the house with a heavy backpack on my back, the aluminum crates of eggs in one hand and a ski pole in my right hand. I had to go alone, since it was time for milking and feeding, the time when Zuck couldn't get away. When we had a hired boy, he would go with me.

But usually I plodded alone through the dark woods, equipped as though for a Lapland expedition: thick wool stockings, inner and outer ski pants, two pairs of socks in felt shoes with felt soles shoved into thigh-high rubber boots, flannel shirt, wool sweater, sheepskin vest, and over it all a fur-lined trench coat with a fur hat and fur gloves. When the northwest wind blew, I wore in addition a woolen helmet over my face that had only slits for my eyes, and I looked in this costume like the Ku Klux Klan incarnate going through the woods.

At the beginning of the path I often had to use a flashlight.

I was afraid of the dark and of the stillness, of the snow which damped all sounds and concealed life and movement alike. I didn't like at all hearing only my own footsteps, the creaking crunch of the rubber boots in the deep holes in the snow. When a tree branch broke under its weight of snow, I was frightened to death.

I was also afraid of the animals in the woods.

When in the first winter a bear chose to make his winter quarters in a fallen tree trunk very near our house, Zuck said that there was nothing to be afraid of—the bear would sleep there peacefully all winter. But I distrusted its sleep and feared its awakening. For my cold comfort I found a fellow in fear in a meter reader from the company that brought electric power to our house. When he found the bear tracks he didn't come back again, and from that hour on he sent a postcard on which we could report our usage ourselves.

When I went through the woods alone and unprotected, and the loneliness pressed heavily on me, I liked to call up a certain picture to my mind.

In it I saw Zuck going ahead of me on the path through the woods, with a lynx on his right and a skunk on his left. Behind him came a whole procession of raccoons, beavers, porcu-

pines, weasels, and snakes, and then a bear came up to him and laid his paw on his shoulder in a friendly fashion . . .

Zuck loved all animals and was not afraid of them. He could share his room with a poisonous spider and a scorpion and live with them in peace. Perhaps this friendly unconcern stemmed from the time in his early youth when he wanted to start out as a tiger trainer and ended up with a mixed group of rabbits and bears.

Even in the first years of our marriage he tried to smuggle snakes into the house, and one time he came home with an Aesculapius adder which had wrapped itself comfortably around his neck. But at that time I didn't want to share our house with snakes and pests, and no suspicion crossed my mind that I would one day have to live with pigs, poultry, rats, and spiders, and with wild animals around the house.

At the corner where the road through the woods came out on the highway, Harry was waiting for me. Rather, I always waited for him. When Harry arrived with predictable lateness, I climbed quickly into my warm car, put all my bundles on the back seat, and changed my rubber boots and felt shoes for lighter footwear, since the gas pedal, clutch, and brakes of my Oldsmobile form a fine-tuned keyboard that doesn't tolerate a heavy touch. A light pressure on these sensitive instruments is enough to speed the car up to sixty miles an hour, a not unhazardous speed on snow and ice.

When, however, my car would not start or keep running, I caught the school bus on the same corner, and it was often driven by Harry's wife. The school bus was a standard station wagon that also served to deliver the mail. This made the trip from our place to town take three to four times longer than it would if traveling unhindered and without stops.

When I climbed into the school bus I found a number of schoolchildren already in it. They were going to high school, a higher continuation of the village school that could be a way to the university.

The boys and girls between thirteen and eighteen years old chattered, quacked, cackled, and crowed like our poultry at feeding time. Many sang and whistled popular tunes, and in between they used exclamations and expressions that the school speech of all lands and dialects use and depend on.

There were words like: solid, oh fine, mean, crazy, gosh, first rate, splendid, etc., words that do not sound really original when used singly, but apparently have the effect of covering the uncertainty and awkwardness of young people protectively by perpetual, rhythmic repetition.

Above this noise, surrounded by this constant, bubbling movement of pushing, thumping, jumping up, and throwing themselves back on the seats, Harry's wife Naoma reigned, broad, powerful, and with indomitable good humor. Along the entire way stood countless mailboxes by the highway. They looked like metal nests for laying hens. Where the highway went through the woods again, there were many lonely mailboxes, as far away from the farms they belonged to as our mailbox at the end of the road through the woods on the corner of the highway, almost a mile and a half from our house.

Only after we returned to Europe did it occur to me how unusual it was that nothing was stolen from these widely separated mailboxes standing by the open highway. At our mailbox treasures such as whiskey, tobacco, meat, coffee, etc., were often deposited by the letter carrier, and in all the years we were there we always found everything just as it had been left.

Europeans would explain this amazing phenomenon by saying that the American people are too well-off to need to bother with such petty thefts.

This inappropriate explanation is surely not the right one. Rather, there is a conviction that petty thievery, useless lies, and intentional distrust are basically antisocial, and they are condemned as an aggravation and burden to daily life.

Indeed, you can sometimes find among the noteworthy items in the newspaper a pointed invitation like this: "Would the person who took the things from the Maple Farm shed without permission please return them and put them on the veranda behind the kitchen to avoid unpleasantness."

Even clearer and more accommodating is this newspaper notice: "Would the girl who was seen taking a blue and white striped shawl from the bench in front of the house please return it to Jim Potwin? It would be appreciated, and no questions will be asked."

From the lonely mailboxes in the woods, that stood there

dumb and silent, we came to the ones near farms, by which farm wives stood and waited for conversation and entertainment.

They gave Naoma commissions and spoke about the events of the day, the weather, and sickness.

In those places where no one was standing Naoma pulled the bags out of the mailboxes that stood on the left-hand side of the road, because she had the driver's seat on the left.

When I sat next to her in the front seat I was allowed to take the mailbags from all the boxes on the right-hand side of the road.

It was done this way: Naoma drove up to within an inch of the mailbox. I reached my arm through the open window, opened the flap door of the mailbox and checked for bags as though I wanted to get an egg from the nest.

Often there was also a slip of paper there with an order that could hardly be deciphered, but Naoma knew her customers and their misspellings.

After that I had to shut the mailbox again and put down the flag that was fastened to the side of the box, a signal that told the owner: "Your mail has been picked up."

These little mail bags, about the size of a Christmas stocking, had shapes and appearances that represented their owners.

There were colorful, friendly bags on which the family name was stitched. There were clean, strong ones in faded gray. There were cheerful, dusty bags with scrawled names, and some that were crushed, crumpled, and dirty, and smelled like moldy bread.

The pauses by the mailboxes were short in comparison with the stops caused by snow and ice in the winter, by mud in the spring, and by storms in the summer.

There was no greater pleasure for the children than to get stuck in the snow, to dance on the ice with the auto, or even to slide off into the ditch.

But I also enjoyed seeing the change in Naoma when she turned from being a simple chauffeur into the helmsman of a ship and issued commands from the bridge to get her ship floating free of the sandbank again. I proposed to her on one of these occasions that right after the end of the war I would send a practical and heart-moving letter to the army about the climate and road conditions of Vermont and suggest using tanks to transport schoolchildren and mail in winter and mud season, a project that should be earnestly considered for the New England states.

In spite of all mishaps, we always got to town sooner or later, and I went from store to store to place the orders which I would pick up on the next day or the day after that.

Eventually the bus came to take me to the train station at a railroad junction town with a main street and shops, a place where that hectic joylessness is found that pervades towns that exist only for getting off, getting on, or changing trains.

In this joyless town, however, is a hotel that is managed by a cheerful, jovial Swiss couple where we establish our assembly point and base camp when we go on trips.

On my trips to the library I made a stop there to rearrange myself, to indulge in a second breakfast, and to overcome the fatigue from the first part of the trip.

The hotel owners kept a room and a bathroom ready for me, and there I could peel myself, layer by layer, like an onion. When I was again wearing normal underwear, skirt, and blouse, and no longer looked like a chestnut vendor in a snowstorm, I felt prepared inwardly and outwardly to enter the hallowed halls of the library.

But every time I began to gather up the pieces of my North Pole outfit and pack it in a bag, the thought of the return journey came to me, and I imagined it in all its terror and had to remember and fear that there could be still more snow, more cold, perhaps even ice.

I saw myself on the return trip, the car loaded down with supplies, with books, with food for the animals, and all the various other things.

I saw Zuck standing on the corner, the big pack basket on his back, the dogs on a leash.

I saw how we pulled all the things out of the car and piled them on the feed sacks and on the toboggan that stood under the mailbox, so that what I had brought would not be harmed by the snow.

Then, when I had taken my own car, we had to drive down the highway to the village to leave the car in Harry's garage. Then we had to walk back along the long highway on foot to

174

the corner in the woods where the load carrying began. The goods were divided among backpacks, pockets, pack basket, and toboggan. I began to mutter softly about why couldn't the wolfhounds be trained like arctic huskies, and why couldn't we harness them to the sled, instead of trudging behind them loaded down like beasts of burden.

In all these years, with fiendish regularity, a strong wind sprang up while we were walking home through the woods and whipped the snow into our faces.

Zuck usually went first and stamped out the way with his heavy boots. I stumbled behind, blinded by the snow, with ice cold fingertips and toes, and rage in my heart.

One time the way home was so bitter that I fell down eighteen times, eleven because the snow gave way, seven from rage. I couldn't curse because I had to clench my teeth together. I couldn't weep because the tears froze to ice and hurt my skin.

Zuck, however, went ahead of me like a mountain guide across a glacier, calmly, carefully, checking the tricky snow with his boots and his ski pole.

Sometimes he turned around, sensing my teeth-clenching desperation from behind, and silently took a couple of packages from me. In bad storms the way from the corner to the house lasted more than an hour, and the light of our house appeared to me like a lighthouse across a heavy sea. When I got inside the house, I put down my burdens in the kitchen and went to the fireplace in the living room.

Zuck threw a few pieces of wood on the fire, and I knelt quite close to the fire and waited until my hands and feet thawed and my rage began to melt and it was time for the evening barn chores.

That was the nightmare of the return trip through snow and wilderness and cold that pursued me even on the outward journey.

But then, when I traveled further toward the university town and saw the top of the library tower appear over the hills, it was all past, and I began to rejoice over the immediate, good present.

I stopped on the main street of the lovely, friendly town and delivered the eggs and poultry.

Then came the last stop, the call to my friends. I let them

know that I had arrived safely and that, late that evening after the library closed, I would come to them. When I climbed back into my car after this call, I had a pleasant anticipation of the close of the day.

I would go to the house of my friends. The house is roomy and bright, and built in Scandinavian–American style. The library is done in almost white natural wood, and the fireplace is made of red tiles.

When I arrive they will still be up.

No one can mix an Old-Fashioned the way he does, the man of the house, and although it is an impossible hour for cocktails, still he brews a mixture of whiskey, bitters, orange rind, and ice and puts a cherry in it.

We say "Good evening" and "Hello" when I walk in, and then we speak without transition about things that are happening to us, near us, and in the world.

We get excited about inadequacies. We look for examples and describe people with their failings and idiosyncrasies. We criticize and express dissatisfaction with current circumstances, but the sphere and angles of these conversations are new and unusual. For behind every criticism the assumption is always there that a change for the better can happen, a change that won't come from common sources, like the government, nor from indefinite sources, like historical developments, but can and will proceed from individuals. After talking with these friends I suddenly feel a personal responsibility, not only for my own fate, but also as a part of the power which produces movement and change. Often we sit late into the night together. Sometimes a phone call interrupts our conversation and demands his services as a doctor, calling him to someone critically ill . . .

After I had called my friends and assured myself of a night's lodging, I drove my car to the west wing of the library, where the cars of the students were parked in long rows.

It was twelve o'clock. The clock in the tower struck, and the bells began their melody for the hour.

I stood in front of the revolving door of the library. As I moved into it, I thought of a revolving stage. Time and place were changing, and a new act began.

The Library

Here is then the library: my rock, my refuge, my cloister. When I sit in my cell, no goat bleats, no chicken cackles, no pig grunts, no duck quacks, no goose honks, no rooster crows.

It has the good smells of leather and dust. It is cool, isolated, and completely quiet.

I am speaking of my own cell on the tenth floor. It takes three keys to get to it. The first key unlocks the elevator that takes me to the ninth floor. This is the place where all religions are brought together. Here the popes stand in long rows, and not far from them is Martin Luther in a splendid edition. Calvin and Zwingli are here, the Mormons and the Shakers. Here also are the church fathers and Buddha, Confucius, the Jews, the saints, and Mohammed. The dogmatists and the heretics are here, the peacemakers and the fighters, the saints and the devils.

Sometimes, when I hurry out through the half darkened corridors of this floor as the closing bell is ringing, it seems to me that they are all trapped in their books by a spell and condemned to frustrated silence.

The second key unlocks the door to the tenth floor at the top of a steep, narrow iron staircase. It leads to a passageway past a long row of studies, small cell-like rooms, each with a large desk, a swivel chair, a bookcase, and a window with a view of the White Mountains of New Hampshire. The third key opens the study door. Each of the fifty-one study rooms has its own individual key. These cubicles are reserved for professors

177

where, we are told, "work can be carried on close to books, and without interruption or disturbance."

On the eighth and ninth floors, the studies are on corridors separated from the rest of the library by an iron grillwork. The tenth floor is given over entirely to study rooms. "The doors to the corridors are kept locked, no telephones are allowed, and typewriters, if any, must be 'noiseless.' These studies are assigned, for the period of a semester, to members of the faculty who seem to have special need of them. Some like to use them because their work requires a large number of books which it would be very uncomfortable to carry home. Others may need fewer books, but they have small children at home, or students come into their offices and interfere seriously with important work they are doing. For all of these a library study can be of inestimable value." After about two years, when I had become a familiar visitor to the library, I received a study room for the first time. I had to use innumerable books at the same time, since my plan was to compare old documents from the early Middle Ages. At home I was seriously disturbed in my work. For me the cubicle was of inestimable value.

Even driving into the town and catching sight of the university gave me, every time, feelings of joy, peace, and content.

The library stands exactly in the middle of the town. It is no accident that it is located there. This central place was chosen deliberately.

On the south side of the library is a broad middle section with two matching wings in Colonial Georgian style, red brick with white window frames and doors and a white tower. Since the library stands on a slope, the north side has ten low floors, while the rest of the building has only two high stories.

The middle section, with its tall church windows and tower, reminds one of the peaceful, square churches of New England.

The building is simple and beautiful in its massive proportions. Although it was built in 1928 in the style of a former era, its effect is genuine and not imitative. It towers over the classroom buildings that surround it on the edge of a grassy lawn with old trees, and it has a commanding situation in the town.

I like best to approach under the trees, past the large playing field, and across the lawn bordered by the three parts of the library. That way I come to the south door, the main library entrance.

I push through the revolving door with my knapsack and pockets full of books and stand in front of the main desk, where books are checked out and returned.

I unpack my books and pile them up. The two pleasant ladies behind the desk take them from me and record their return.

In the first year there was not much conversation, but now I know all the staff by name, and they know me. In time I have even come to know the lady in charge of circulation. There is something in her manner which commands respect, and I always feel a little tempted to curtsy like a schoolgirl in her presence. But when, after three years, she showed me the dumb waiter, the little elevator that you can use to transport your books to any floor instead of carrying them up the stairs yourself, in that memorable moment I felt for the first time that I belonged. I had risen from apprentice to journeyman.

The ladies and I speak about the weather, about our health, about the flowers on the desk, always new and unusually beautiful, about the last concert in Hanover, about happenings in the town. We speak in whispers, though no one is reading in the great hall, because there is something solemn about the hall that allows only muted voices.

Even the students, who have just been romping like St. Bernards and Great Danes on the playing field, come through the hall on tiptoe like the tame bears you feed sugar to, and they buzz like muted trumpets.

This is the enormous entrance hall, long and high like a church. In the middle is the circulation desk, and on the wall behind it is an inscription: "This building is the gift of George F. Baker in memory of his uncle, Fisher Ames Baker, Dartmouth 1859, a soldier in the Civil War and an eminent member of the New York Bar."

George F. Baker gave a million dollars for building the library in 1928, and then donated another million to maintain it. Another former Dartmouth student, Edwin S. Sanborn, class of 1878, left the library a million dollars to buy books, so its excellence seems assured for many years to come.

If it should ever start to decline, other Dartmouth graduates will be found who will gladly reach deep into their pockets to save and preserve the dreams of their youth and the center of their happiest memories.

179

Crimson curtains hang at the great windows of the hall. Large red leather armchairs are provided for those who are waiting or who wish to look through books.

In the east wing of the hall, which has its own door, books of special or current interest are spread on tables. These books may deal, for example, with the causes of the Chinese revolution, atomic energy, the state of cancer research, new novels in world literature, American politics, or modern poetry.

The most recent books are at the circulation desk itself. These may usually be borrowed for only three hours and read only in the library, because many readers are waiting for them.

There are glass cases built into the north wall of the hall, where pictures and books of special interest are displayed. In the west wing of the hall stands the card catalog, arranged by author on the left side and by subject on the right for those who have forgotten the author of a book or want to have a complete bibliography of a subject.

From the east wing of the entrance hall you can reach two large rooms. One is the plain but friendly room which is only for newspapers. Across from it is the reference room, paneled in gray-green wood, with highly polished dark tables and antique chairs. Alcoves and bookcases are built into the walls, and it looks like a library in an English castle, where the lord really reads the books he owns.

This is the place for dictionaries, encyclopedias, bibliographies, and atlases. Grimm's dictionary is there, and another dictionary that gives terms for food in six languages. There are collections of quotations and genealogies, "Who's Who" books for the living and the dead. The library handbook tells me that the volumes in this room are books that give the answers to the questions most often asked in university libraries.

The desk at the front of the reference room is manned by staff members from 8:00 A.M. until 11:00 P.M. There are small forms for inquiries, and the librarians, always friendly and helpful, give out information tirelessly. They help the students look for titles in the card catalog and find books on the shelves. They help them find material on the Emperor Augustus or Churchill. They tell them where to put their coats, where they may smoke, and where they may not.

"Although the privilege of smoking is practically never accorded in libraries because of the hazard of fire," the handbook states, "yet in accordance with the idea of making the Baker Library an enjoyable place in which to study, smoking is permitted in the Tower Room, the seminar rooms on the top floor, and the northeast study room in the basement. Students are asked to confine their smoking to these three places."

The Tower Room, which can be reached by two big staircases from the entrance hall, takes up the whole second floor. It is a gigantic room, oak-paneled, with large and small tables and comfortable armchairs. Here, they say, students should read for pleasure, and not because of tests and grades. The chairs are durable but not too massive, and so comfortable that you often hear the students snoring in rows. Especially during the war you could often hear a powerful many-voiced chorus of snores, because nine-tenths of the students were in the navy and had to get up by six, and this was the only undisturbed place where they could rest.

In this room, which holds about four thousand books, there are all kinds of reading to bring students in contact with "the best of modern creative work as well as with the great minds of the past; with humor, light fiction, adventure, as much as with serious thought."

"No rules or restrictions are posted here," they explain. "It is assumed that this room and its contents will be regarded as one would the library of one's club. It is possible that in later years some students may feel that in this room were spent some of the most valued hours of their college life." On winter evenings faculty members sometimes read aloud poems and prose here. The students gather about the fire that burns in the fireplace. Soft lamplight fills the room, and over everything spreads the fragrance of coffee, which is served in the background. "If the library is in a certain sense the heart of the college," they say, "this room is the heart of the library."

There are many other rooms in the library, for example the places where books are sorted and catalogued. There is also a room where the catalogs of Harvard Library and the Library of Congress are kept. If a book is not in the Dartmouth Library, it can be borrowed from Harvard, Yale, the Library of Congress, or some other library.

There is a staff of employees whose job it is to get the book you need. In all the five years I used the library, I never heard, "That book is not available. I cannot get it for you."

Once I asked for a remarkable book about the childhood of the monk Benedict and his sister Scholastica. I emphasized that the book was not absolutely necessary, but because of its uniqueness I would like to see it. The search took two months, but finally they found it in a Benedictine monastery in Indiana. When it arrived I had to pay only the postage, here and back, eighty cents. There was no borrowing fee. "No limit is set to the number of books a person can borrow," they explain. "Some books are known to be peculiarly difficult to replace if lost, and students are requested to use these only in the library. . . . Students are allowed to keep books for two weeks with the privilege of renewal unless others are asking for them."

In November 1946, before I left for Europe, I brought back sixty-eight books, and many of them I had had for three months or longer. Of course most of them were about the early Middle Ages, a subject not of interest to many readers. There is a fine for overdue books of three cents and five cents a day. "The system breaks down if books are not returned so that others may use them. Fines are not imposed to make money or even primarily to inflict a penalty. . . . Most failures to return are due to thoughtlessness, and the fines are imposed, and made large, to help prevent this."

Most of the books are in excellent condition. This is not the result of special carefulness on the part of the students, but because the books are taken to the bindery in the cellar before they fall apart, and then they reappear in new bindings.

In the library is also a museum, a small room patterned after the first library, founded in 1772 by Bezaleel Woodward, a mathematics professor and the first librarian.

There is also a Treasure Room which contains rare books. It is a solemn, empty, elegant room. Its stained glass windows are decorated with mottoes and crests that have to do with the history and traditions of the university. Somewhere I once read in a description of this room: "A question has been raised about the significance of the three stars pictured on one of the windows. It should be stated here that they are the original seal of the Phi Beta Kappa society of Dartmouth and have no connection with the trademark of Hennessy cognac."

Right next to this room are the offices of the library staff and the head librarian, rooms so fine and comfortable that you wonder if they ever want to go home.

One of the librarians, Mr. Rugg, collects unusual plants, and his office looks like an exotic greenhouse. When I wanted to do a particular historical study and needed help, I was introduced to him, and he gave me a tour of the library.

I later received two letters from him, which I have saved. One is dated January 1942, five weeks after the outbreak of war, and says, "I heard yesterday that you are having difficulty in coming over to Hanover because of the new government regulations. I hope that these problems can be cleared up, and that you can get permission to come to the library. In the meantime, if you need particular books, please send me a list, and I will be glad to have them sent to you. You need pay only the postage for them. With friendliest greetings to you both. . ."

The second letter came six months later, when we had very strict gas rationing that kept us from traveling far. "I haven't seen you since gas rationing went in," he wrote, "and I hope that you have received a supplementary card so that you can continue your studies at the library. Some of my friends have been promised supplementary cards for doing research. Meanwhile we will of course be glad to send you the books you need by mail."

In the meantime, however, I received a supplementary ration card as a farmer because I began to sell eggs, goat milk, chickens, ducks, and geese in Hanover. I set my sales location near the library, and Mr. Rugg was pleased and satisfied.

In 1943, in the middle of the war, when I received permission to accompany an American friend on her 3,000-mile trip clear across the country to California, I sent Mr. Rugg a redwood root from San Francisco. It was a little root of one of the giant trees of the western forests. Tunnels large enough for auto traffic are cut through their trunks. They grow over one hundred thirty feet high and live to the venerable age of nine hundred or more years. Whether this little scion of a giant tree has taken root in Mr. Rugg's eastern garden, or perhaps in a flower pot in his office, I haven't asked. Possibly, when I come back, I will see the beginning of a tree, for Mr. Rugg is a magician with plants, as well as having a good hand for books.

Downstairs there is also a section of medical books, a photostat copying room, and a large room under the entrance hall where students can read specially assigned books. The walls of this room are covered with paintings by a modern Mexican artist. We are told to have patience and to study them thoroughly before rejecting them. I have studied them thoroughly, but I have little patience, and I avoid this room. All the rooms that I have described are for getting books, for studying and thinking, or for relaxing.

But there is still the core of the library, made up of the nine levels where the books are kept. The Americans call these "stacks," a word that means to arrange in layers, heap or pile up, and is sometimes used in connection with piles of bricks or hay in barns.

You go to these stacks to look for books. The process is very simple. In the card catalog in the entrance hall you look under the title or the author of the book you want. Then you write down the call number on a slip of paper, perhaps H 26 R 322C. Next to the door leading into the stacks is a large directory sign, where you can see that H (History) is on the sixth level, while 26 indicates which bookcase holds the book. R is the first letter of the author's name, and 322C is the number of the book on the shelf and indicates further that it is the so-and-so-many-eth book by the same author. Sometimes you find the letter "q" or "f" on the catalog card. That means: Look out! This book is of unusual size, quarto or folio, and will be on a special shelf big enough to hold such books. In addition, there are directories by each of the stairways, in case you forget what you read on the large directory sign at the entrance.

Since the library stands on a slope, as I mentioned before, you come from the entrance hall, which seems to be at ground level, into the fourth floor of the stacks. There are three levels of stacks below, three above. Each level is eight feet high, and on the right and left are stairs connecting the levels. On each level there are three corridors, two wide ones which are lighted by a row of windows where there are desks and tables, and a narrow one in the middle between the bookshelves. These corridors are like three parallel roads, connected by eleven crossroads lined with books on dark green iron shelves from floor to ceiling. On the end of every bookcase are again numbers showing what books are to be found there and indicating precisely the geometric position of every volume. The middle corridors and the alleys between the shelves are illuminated by many electric lights that you turn on yourself and should turn off as you leave. On the north wall of every level are seven open cubicles with tables and chairs where you can look over the books or read them before checking them out and taking them home. On the second and third levels the cubicles are closed for students who want to concentrate on their work and study without interruption. Finding books is not difficult after you master the system. But then comes the best part — the book you are looking for is surrounded by books you didn't know about, or have forgotten, or that you perhaps knew once and now find again.

Sometimes, when I had worked in my room on the tenth level for eight or nine hours and was tired, I went down and wandered through the avenues and alleyways of books, stopped where I wanted to, drew out a book, leafed through it, and laid it on one of the tables so that I could look into it again when I pleased.

Books that have been taken from the shelves should be piled up on tables so that they can be replaced correctly by trained hands and not exposed to the danger of accidental misplacing. Every morning a staff of young people is busy putting books back in the places where they belong so that they can be found again.

So I go through the stacks, look at the books, taste many, and sometimes find a new friend. And as I go through the rows of hundreds of thousands of books, I think these are all mine to use. These belong to me, to the students, to the professors, and to the visitors who come to the library. It is this feeling of common property, or of the possession of the unusual by the common people, that underlies the fact that hardly anyone wants to take anything away and keep it. Theft is not a problem in the library and does not have to be taken into consideration. In my rounds I go down to the third and fourth stacks, where the alleyways are lit by bluish fluorescent lights on the ceilings.

Here are the Greeks and Romans, the old geographers that

reported about the Island of Thule and the Amazons. Here stagecoach travelers tell about the Alps, rickshaw travelers about China, and flyers about the South Pole. Here is the fall of Rome and the rise of Christianity. Here are the biographies, from Alexander the Great to Bernard Shaw and Franklin D. Roosevelt. Here are the Russians in their anarchist and religious, Christian and terrorist, pacifist and revolutionary writers, represented up to the recent Soviet comedies and plays. Here is Shakespeare in old and new editions, in all interpretations, appearing in all his different characters. Here are the English, from Beowulf to Priestley.

Here are the Germans, from the Ulfilas Bible through the editions of classical and romantic writers to Barlach's "Blauer Boll." No stop is made with the modern writers. They stream in, newer and newer, without end or censorship.

In the fall of 1945, Nazi books arrived: novels, magazines, schoolbooks, poetry. They were sorted and set out. A small display of them was put together in the glass cases in the entrance hall. There were no propagandists among them, no goose-step display. They were legitimate books like *Mein Kampf,* a Rosenberg, a Ludendorf, poems by Schirach, photographs of the Führer, German magazine pictures of the war. The aggressive titles, the ugly Führer, the poor-quality printing all drew amazed comments and derision from the students. In another case were pictures from German magazines, mostly nature shots, and they called forth admiration.

The books are all here, the Americans, the French, the Scandinavians, the Dutch, and the Italians, the Russians, the Indians, the Chinese, and the Spanish. Here are the masses of people of all eras in their literature and their history. Here are religion, law, music, folklore, the sciences, agriculture, fishing and hunting, sports, technology, detective stories. Everything is arranged, but not abridged and not selected. The students to whom this library has been given are to search, choose, and decide for themselves what they want to do with it. The older generation does not want to rule the younger, and the young people do not fear their elders.

When the Dartmouth College library was dedicated, the librarian made a speech:

Every achievement of the human spirit is based chiefly on faith.

Those who planned this library planned it with faith, they worked into its very fabric certain beliefs which *none* can prove, which I will not argue.

They believed that more and more Dartmouth will teach that all things are interlocked about a central reality. Therefore they planned to place the building so that it might be at the heart of the campus, yet so that related buildings could be grouped about it; to draw in all the books of the college; to keep the books for the most part central in the building, and not dispersed.

They believed that to surround boys with beauty is good—a part of their education. Therefore, of certain rooms, the design, color, and furnishings were studied as problems in the creation of beauty.

They believed that students should be given a chance to acquire the habit of reading, as a resource for leisure, as the surest way to retain a keen and useful mind; therefore, the Tower Reading Room is an experiment in the cultivation of the reading habit.

Of the background of these beliefs — of a central reality of beauty, of the best of the heritage of the past — the tower is the symbol, for Dartmouth an inspiration, for the world a sign.

Vox Clamantis in Deserto

One day I went to the reference desk and asked what the weather vane on the tower meant.

I had regarded it for a long time as an unusual rooster with bristling feathers and without a head.

They showed me the bookplate of the library books, and at the same time I learned a few things about the founding and history of Dartmouth College, a remarkable and unique story.

As soon as I looked at the bookplate I saw that it was the same scene as the one on the weather vane.

There is a pine, forty feet tall, and under it is a cask, and next to the cask is a tree stump, and on the tree stump sits a man. The man has on buckled shoes and a long coat, and his long hair is tied back. He has raised his right arm and holds up the index finger of his right hand. In his index finger is not the inflexibility of a warning about or against something. In its position (one might almost call it movement, even though it is cast in iron), in the gesture of his arm and hand, which extends from a large sleeve with a wide cuff, but above all in his index finger lies the wagging, illustrating, expansive gesture of teaching.

In front of him sits a strange pupil. He squats on the ground with crossed legs. On his head are two feathers, and he has in his mouth a long pipe, which he holds with both hands, as though he wanted to play the flute.

This is the iron weather vane of Dartmouth. The seal of Dartmouth has, however, this inscription: vox clamantis in deserto.

188

And this is the history of Dartmouth, as I heard it, and as I read it. It belongs so much to the land and people, and is so much bound up with our landscape, the severity of the weather, the perseverance and tenacity of the people, that I want to report it as proof and example of everything that I have told so far.

There was a man, and his name was Eleazar Wheelock, a well-known pulpit orator, pamphleteer, polemicist, and above all the founder and owner of a school for Indians in the state of Connecticut.

His dream, his wish, and his goal were to some extent uncommon: he wanted, instead of attacking, demoralizing, or killing the original inhabitants of America, to civilize, educate, and teach them.

His plans were not limited to founding a school in which the Indians could be taught the ABC's, Christianity, and to sit on benches. Mr. Wheelock's plan was no more and no less than to create a college, a real university, for Indians and whites.

How the money for it was raised, how the location for the college was found, and in what way it developed comprises one of the most unusual histories of a place of higher education.

In the founding documents of Dartmouth is written:

> In the name of King George we do of our special grace, certain knowledge and mere motion, ordain, grant & constitute that there be a college erected in our said province of New Hampshire by the name of Dartmouth College for the education & instruction of Youth of the Indian Tribes in this Land in reading, writing & all parts of Learning which shall appear necessary and expedient for civilizing & christianizing Children of Pagans as well as in all liberal Arts and Sciences; and also of English Youth and any others, . . . and not excluding any Person of any religious denomination whatsoever from free & equal liberty & advantage of Education or from any of the liberties and privileges or immunities of the said College on account of his or their speculative sentiments in Religion, & of his or their being of a religious profession different from the said Trustees of the said Dartmouth College.

First must be reported how the money was raised to make it possible to found a university.

Mr. Eleazar Wheelock had friends in New England who were enthusiastic about the pious plan to convert and educate the wild Indians.

The main plan consisted of winning over the powerful Earl of Dartmouth and securing his help. The two emissaries Mr. Wheelock chose to send to England were an unusual pair.

One was Nathaniel Whitaker, a handsome, tall, and stately man, a pugnacious champion of God with an unbendable will and potent stubbornness, a Presbyterian from Princeton College.

The other emissary was Samuel Occom, a full-blooded Indian from the tribe of the Mohicans in Connecticut.

It took forty-five days for the two to get to England. Bad storms delayed their journey, and they finally reached London the evening of February 6, 1766.

The sensation that they aroused was enormous, but, as far as Occom's diaries report, he didn't notice the excitement that he caused, or it made no impression on him. Samuel Occom went with the feather-light step of the Indian in woods and prairies through the streets of London. His smooth black hair fell over his shoulders onto his black clerical garb, and his copper-colored face rose calm and unmoved from the dark priestly garment with its white bands under the chin.

Indeed, the sensation that he made was so great that he was soon thereafter portrayed in the theater in a comedy, something which amazed him.

The only thing that made an impression on Occom was the wild activity in London on the holy Sabbath day, and he wrote about it in his diary: "Last Sabbath Evening I walk'd with Mr. Whitaker to Cary a letter to my Lord Dartmouth and Saw Such Confution as I never dreamt of, there was some at Churches Singing and Preaching, in the Streets Some Cursing, Swearing and Damming one another, others was holloaing, Whestling, talking, gigling, and Laughing, and Coaches and footmen passing and repassing, Crossing and Cress-Crossing, and the poor Begers Praying Crying and Beging up on their Knees."

The success of Occom, the Indian in clerical garb, was decisive.

Lord Dartmouth received him and undertook the patronage

of the future university, gave it his name, and started the subscription list with fifty pounds.

Reverend Whitaker, who had a good head for advertising, did the organizing, and Occom preached. He preached in England from more than three hundred pulpits. It is said that he even preached before the king. Whether this really happened is not certain, but it is well documented that the king donated two hundred pounds.

Occom, it is said, preached with the natural eloquence and vividness of the redskin. He drew a visionary picture of the great conversion of all the Indian tribes, and his listeners donated money and gave gifts and helped him in his mission.

The gifts came from all levels of society, from the king to the peasant. There were rich, eccentric merchants, like fat Mr. Thornton, who later gave Mrs. Wheelock a state carriage so that she could drive through the wilderness in style.

There were people who were entered in the lists in the following manner:

1 widow 5 shillings

2 widows 16 shillings 2 pence.

There were, however, also setbacks. The Archbishop of Canterbury said, "as the Dissenters did not help us, neither will we help them," and Whitaker reported that the Bishop of Gloucester "would not give us a penny nor ask us to sit down!"

Finally they had a list with 2,500 names on it, and as the two emissaries reached America again two years later in April 1768, they brought with them, to the glory of God and for the good of the Indians, eleven thousand pounds, an uncommonly large amount in those times.

Meanwhile, Mr. Wheelock had been looking for a piece of land in America. He did not want to stay in the state of Connecticut, since he held that it was wiser to begin the new school in the wilderness, in the midst of the Indians' accustomed surroundings.

The road of suffering that Mr. Wheelock now had to traverse, the animosity which he met, the scorn and the setbacks, a less single-minded and stubborn man could not have borne. But Mr. Wheelock must have been that type of New Englander that cannot be bent or broken.

In 1765 Governor Wentworth of New Hampshire had

promised him five hundred acres of land.

In 1770 matters were far enough along for Wheelock to undertake an eight-week journey into the northern woods in the spring to find the right place for his university. When he had found the right place, a storm of indignation broke around him from those who had thought of a different place or those who thought they had been overlooked in the choice of location.

Wheelock was pointed out, insulted, and slandered as a fantasist and traitor who was interested only in his own gain. His answer was: "The site for Dartmouth College was not determined by any private interest or party on earth, but was the Redeemer's choice."

With that it should be noted that the first president of Dartmouth College was of the unalterable opinion that he and the Almighty stood on such excellent footing that no power on earth could ever come between them.

At the beginning of August, Eleazar Wheelock got under way and took with him a couple of workmen, a loaded oxcart, one teacher, and one student northward along the Connecticut River, over which there were no bridges, and which had to be crossed in Indian canoes.

This trip through the wilderness was later put into song by a Dartmouth student, who made the historical error of believing that the keg of rum was in Mr. Wheelock's baggage, while it was actually transported later in Mrs. Wheelock's caravan. The verse runs:

"Oh, Eleazar Wheelock was a very pious man:
He went into the wilderness to teach the Indian,
With *Gradus ad Parnassum,* a *Bible* and a drum,
And five hundred gallons of New England rum."

Mr. Wheelock and his company fought their way through the thick forest along the wearisome paths, and it was a great effort to reach their chosen place through the mountainous land.

There on a high plateau stood, it is reported, forty-foot-tall pines, a forest so dense that the sun could not shine on the floor except at midday when it stood at the zenith. However, the tall trees also kept the storms off, and in the dimness of the forest, they say, it was as still as in a cathedral. Only the growling of

192

bears, the howling of wolves, the screaming and crying of lynxes, and the snarling of panthers sometimes broke the stillness.

If the good Doctor Wheelock, they tell, had wanted a quiet place for his college, a place far distant from the temptations of the populous cities, he could scarcely have found a quieter or more remote one.

Three weeks later a blockhouse stood on the cleared land, twenty feet square, with windows of isinglass and waxed paper, and the men began to prepare quarters for the students. In the middle of September, six weeks after Mr. Wheelock's departure, Mrs. Wheelock started off.

She rode in the lordly state carriage which had been given her by the English merchant; it was drawn by two disgruntled, panting horses.

Behind the coach came the oxcart, loaded with a barrel of salt pork, a half barrel of sugar, wine, tobacco, pipes, and other provisions, but above all with the fabled keg of rum.

In her train marched the four Negro slaves of the Wheelock family: Exeter, Brister, Chloe, and Peggy. Behind them came a cow that belonged to Brister, who had stubbornly refused to go without Peggy and the cow even though it was highly questionable whether there would be enough feed for the cow.

Behind them came thirty students, Indian and white. Horses, oxen, and men trotted, plodded, and stumbled along the bumpy, almost impassable road. It must have taken not a little effort to keep the kegs from rolling off the oxcart, to say nothing of Mrs. Wheelock, who was shaken, jolted, rattled, and thrown about in her state carriage like a sailor in a storm on the high seas.

The caravan could only cover a few miles a day. At the beginning of their trip a messenger came riding to meet them, a teacher sent by Mr. Wheelock, who urged them to turn back at once. A shortage of water had occurred, and Mr. Wheelock had to find new springs before he could prepare comfortable lodgings for Mrs. Wheelock and the students.

Water or no water, Mrs. Wheelock could not be persuaded to turn back, and nothing in the world could stop her from traveling on. So, for the disappointed messenger, who had ridden night and day and had a special dispensation in his pocket that stated that he might proceed even on the Sabbath, there remained nothing to do but to turn his horse and accompany the slow procession on its weary way through the wilderness.

The arrival of the caravan meant for Mr. Wheelock and his helpers complete confusion and the upsetting of all plans. But since in every mishap, accident, or good fortune he saw the hand of the Lord, he did not despair.

He quartered his wife and the female members of the train in the finished blockhouse without water, and built, with the help of the Indians, temporary shelters for himself, his sons, the servants, and the students. When soon after that a new group of students and teachers arrived from Boston, the situation became even worse. A teacher gave the following description of their circumstances:

> It was near the close of the day. There was scanty room in the Doctor's shanty for the shelter of those who were on the ground, and none for us who had just arrived. All constructed for a temporary residence a tent of crotched stakes and poles covered with boughs. It was soon ready, and we camped down wrapped in our blankets, and for a time slept very comfortably. During the night, however, a storm arose of high wind and pelting rain. Our tent came down and buried us in its ruins. After mutual inquiry, we found no one injured, and as the storm raged without abated fury, we resolved to abide the issue as we were, and wait for the day. When fair weather returned, we made more substantial booths for our protection till better accommodations could be provided.

By the beginning of the winter there were two blockhouses. One housed the classrooms and the Wheelock family. The other, which was larger and more comfortable, was inhabited by the servants and the cow. Around them huts were built for the students. The roof of the college building was not quite finished when the first snow fell.

In this first winter they were often hungry. The most important staples had to be brought sixty miles through snow and mud on bad roads, or be towed in from landings on the river, over waterfalls, cliffs, and through the dense forest. Some students left that winter, but most remained and studied.

During the next spring a large house with two stories was built. It had a hall, a kitchen, and sixteen rooms for the stu-

194

dents. A barn was added, a wash house and a cook house, and on the newly cleared land cultivation was begun.

In the summer of 1771 — after one year — the place in the primeval forest looked like a university town.

In this first summer of its existence the university held its first final examinations and its first graduation. It was a great occasion.

Governor Wentworth came with sixty gentlemen and brought a silver punchbowl with the necessary rum for it. In addition, he contributed an ox, which was roasted on a spit. The rum flowed in rivers.

Only a so immovably God-fearing man as Mr. Wheelock could have withstood this day of the highest fulfillment of his dreams and of his deepest despair.

You see, Mrs. Wheelock was sick and in bed when the guests arrived, and the cook used this excuse to drink himself unconscious. So Mr. Wheelock had to help in the kitchen himself to prepare the meal for the illustrious guests. He also had to apologize because the college had only one tablecloth that had been given by a charitable lady in Connecticut, and the lack of tablecloths had been taken especially amiss by the farmers and villagers, who apparently felt that it was degrading. All in all, in spite of this, the celebration was remarkably successful.

The first four students were graduated as bachelors of liberal arts.

The program was as follows:

1. An introductory speech about virtues in English, followed by a hymn.

2. A speech about history, delivered in Latin.

3. A disputation in logic, in which a student had to address the question: Can true knowledge of nature be received by divine inspiration? This question was argued by three students.

4. A farewell address in Latin, with a closing hymn that had been composed by the students themselves.

The conclusion was said to be so moving that many of the listeners burst into tears, although up to this point no rum had yet been served from the silver bowl.

The students gave their speeches and disputations from a platform built of rough tree trunks and reached by a plank of unplaned pine.

One of the students, an Indian, refused to use this stage, but climbed to a wide branch of a tall pine and gave his speech from up there with an Indian accent. The first college year ended under a lucky star, so that Mr. Wheelock could send a prospectus for the next year, in which among other things stood: "The Rev. Dr. Wheelock, through the surprising smiles of Heaven upon his unwearied endeavors, has now so nearly effected his great and arduous undertaking to settle and accommodate his Indian school and college in a howling wilderness that he has the fairest prospect in a little time to be able to support an hundred Indian and English youths."

In spite of this success, the school in the wilderness still had many dangers to overcome.

The source of money in England was drying up; the students revolted against the bad food; parents wrote threatening letters about moldy bread, rotten potatoes, and stinking meat. Mr. Wheelock's cooks were a test of his endurance. They stole and had an unquenchable thirst for rum. The greatest thorns in his flesh, however, were the taverns which had sprung up in the town around the college.

It was strictly forbidden for the students to go into the taverns, but they did so anyway, and from that situation came the following dialogue, so terribly painful for Mr. Wheelock, which has been preserved for us.

A student stood before Mr. Wheelock.

"Ah, Miles!" Mr. Wheelock is supposed to have said, and this was set down by that same Miles word for word. "Ah, Miles! it is you. But where is your chum? I sent for him; why does he not come?" "Sir, he is not able to come." "But he can walk, can he not?" "Sir, he cannot stand upon his feet." "Indeed, then he is badly done up. This is a miserable affair. That tavern is a nuisance. But can you tell me, Miles, whether my sons Eleazar and James were there?" "Sir, I understand that they were." "Ah! I suspected it. Bad boys of mine! I have some hopes of James yet; but as to Eleazar he will be damned, I believe."

In spite of all these hard trials and challenges, Dartmouth College prospered.

Two years after its founding it had fifty students, among them six Indians. After four years it already had a hundred students, with twenty-one Indians among them, and in the next year it was praised in Connecticut as the best college on the continent.

Then came Canadian Indians, who were much more difficult to tame than the tribes with which Wheelock was used to dealing. They came and went, turned up and disappeared into the woods again when civilization was too much for them. They disturbed the other students with continuous, shrill howling and by following their inclination for "large beer," as they called it.

Then came a hazardous epoch for the young college: the War of Independence.

The college owed its existence to English money, and its subscribers and protectors were Englishmen. But Mr. Wheelock did not hesitate for a moment and wrote to his English sponsor Thornton—the rich merchant who had given him the state carriage—a letter that stirred the Englishman to a towering fury, but which set Mr. Wheelock in a place of high honor in the history of Dartmouth:

> I believe there never was a more dutiful, loyal, and well-affected people to Government than has ever been in these colonies till the Stamp Act. And the colonies have ever been propense to peace and reconciliation till those horrid murders and savage butcheries, so inhumanly committed under pretence of reducing rebels to obedience. The wringing of the nose bringeth forth blood. Our liberties were dearly bought, and we have tasted the sweetness of them, and esteem them our birthright; and perhaps his Majesty will find they will not be given up so tamely as he imagines. The colonies seem to be determined they will not be slaves.

Wheelock's sons and a few students fought in Washington's army, but otherwise the college suffered little from the war, and studies and graduations went on undisturbed.

Many Indian students disappeared and did not come back and probably fought with their tribes. However, the college had no Indian attacks to endure, although Royalton in Vermont, a place that lies scarcely fifteen miles distant from the college, was at this time plundered, burned, and robbed, and the women and children were murdered, scalped, or carried away into captivity.

197

This Royalton, a half hour from Dartmouth College by car, is still today an uncanny place whose deathly stillness and gloominess make one think of ghosts even at bright noonday.

The Indians spared the college, and the war spared it, since it lay outside the war zone. In addition, Lord Dartmouth had brought the college especially to the attention of the British General Howe and his brother Admiral Howe and had specially urged them to spare it.

The attack at Bunker Hill on June 16, 1775, was heard in peaceful Dartmouth in an unusual way.

In Wheelock's diary is found the entry: "June 16 — The noise of cannon supposed to be at Boston, was heard all day. 17th — The same reports of cannon. We wait with impatience to hear the occasion and the event."

Boston lies three and a half hours from Dartmouth College by express train, but Wheelock's entries were surely not added at a later time.

The thunder of the cannons was heard.

It was heard by one of the Indian students, named Daniel Simons, who lay on the ground and pressed his ear to the earth.

There is much more that could be told about the history of Dartmouth, about the famous men who studied there, about its destinies and battles, about its part in the Civil War — up to the present day, when it is one of the best and, I think, one of the loveliest universities in the country.

At last report it had 3,200 students.

There are no more Indians. The last Indian student, a Sioux, graduated in 1891 and became a famous doctor and author.

There is no more wilderness, and everything is well arranged, prosperous, comfortable, and secure.

But still today Mr. Wheelock sits with his raised index finger in the weathervane high above everything. It is the same Mr. Wheelock of whom they say that when he loved someone, he kept his trust forever, and those whom he did not love he hated like the devil. That is Mr. Wheelock, who, when he was sick and tired, longed for a small pension that would enable him to have some coffee, chocolate, tea, and a small glass of wine, but who nevertheless taught until the hour of his death and died standing.

It is Mr. Wheelock, on whose gravestone is written:

"By the Gospel he subdued the ferocity of the savage;
And to the civilized he opened new paths of science.
Traveller,
Go, if you can, and deserve
The sublime reward of such merit."

The Journey to America

In August 1946 we received the news that Zuck was to begin his government service.

He worked for two months in an office in New York, a branch of the War Department.

Some weekends he spent on the farm, visits that were like military leaves.

We didn't know when he would be sent to Europe. Every visit at the farm could be the last before he was sent over.

We began to say goodbye.

We had been on the farm for five years, and there were many things to consider, practical decisions to make, preparations to take care of.

The house was winterized as usual. We didn't sell the animals, but gave them to a reliable farmer who would keep, shelter, and feed them until our return.

Zuck had signed up for only one year. During this time I was to travel to Europe, first of all to Switzerland. Michi was married and living in the South. Winnetou was studying in California. I could not stay on the farm alone.

So my trip to Europe was my next problem, especially since Zuck's play, which he had somehow managed to finish in the rare pauses during three years of farm work, was to be presented on the stage in Zurich. We agreed that we would all meet again on the farm after a year, but we felt in our bones that it was a final leave-taking.

We felt like Sinbad the Sailor, Gulliver, or the first rocket travelers to Mars.

We imagined the destruction and the terrible conditions over there. We were set to find fewer of our friends and to meet and be strangers, and we had no false illusions.

At the beginning of November, Zuck was suddenly called and sent by airplane to Berlin.

At the end of November I embarked for Holland. It was very difficult to get a berth on a ship, but as luck would have it, I found a place on a Dutch ship that was the sister ship of the one that brought us to America seven years earlier. That one had been sunk by the Japanese, but the surviving sister ship was so like it that I could find my way around immediately, and in a strange way the crossing resembled the one of seven years before. I set out from our landing place in Hoboken, and I arrived at Rotterdam, our earlier point of departure.

It was a slow ship that took nine days to cross. On five different evenings a notice appeared, written with white chalk on the blackboard: "Today at midnight the clock will be set ahead one hour."

The crossing was rather quiet. The ship hammered its way through the water like one of the great plows that tear up the ground in the endless cornfields of the Midwest.

We put thousands of miles behind us and became accustomed to setting the clock and impressing the new time on our minds.

One night I woke up frightened by the stillness. The hammering of the engines had stopped. I saw lights through the cabin porthole. We were in port.

In Rotterdam I saw the first bombed-out houses. Brownish grass grew over the places where the earth had been leveled. There for the first time, too, I saw hunger in the eyes, faces, and skin of the people.

I stayed for a few days with friends in Amsterdam.

That was a proper introduction to later experiences. My Dutch friends had suffered much, but had with difficulty resisted and survived.

Their house had not been damaged, and they had not been injured.

I remembered them as people of unusual beauty, a beauty they showed in every word and movement. They were like pictures that one would like to see again unchanged.

Since it was not a question of separation in the usual sense in these years, we had unconsciously put our memories away in safe places and protected them from our feelings because we had to. The pictures, images, and mementos of our friends had been walled into deep vaults which were later sometimes buried under rubble or lava.

Now the first excavated figures stood before me, the first friends seen after they were brought back to the light. They were undamaged and unchanged. At the most they had a little mortar in one ear, a few grains of sand in the corner of an eye, a small bit of cement in the corner of a mouth.

But nothing was crumbled, nothing had been broken, and the patina of the weathering process they had endured had only heightened their fragile attractiveness.

On December 5, 1946, I arrived at the Swiss border.

At that time American citizens needed not only a visa, but also a valid reason for visiting Switzerland to enter the country.

I had given as the true and important reason for my visit that I was to attend the world premiere of Zuck's new play. I had, however, not inspected my passport, nor looked more closely at the Swiss visa. It was only when I saw the expression on the face of the customs official that I realized that something might not be in order. He went through the whole passport, studying every page. Finally he brought the page with the Swiss visa up quite close to his glasses, and then looked at me questioningly. He read it again, shaking his head. Finally he stamped the page and gave the passport back to me.

On that page, under "Reason for Travel," stood in neat handwriting "Des Teufels General" (The Devil's General).

The premiere performance of *Des Teufels General* took place a week later.

Zuck had received ten days of Christmas leave and arrived from Germany at the last moment with the dirty luggage of a soldier, and with the gray appearance of someone who had just come out of the trenches.

Now we sat in a box at the theater. We heard Zuck's written

202

words speak, saw his figures act, and I had a vision behind it all of Zuck's room in Barnard, Vermont. I heard the noise of his typewriter and the rustling of the paper being added to the piles in the drawer or crumpled into balls and thrown into the wastebasket.

The play was a tremendous success.

Then everything slowly fell into place.

When we were married twenty-three years earlier, Zuck owned two suits and a pile of debts, and I had two dresses and a lampshade.

Six months later Zuck had his first great success, and after a year we had a house in the country, an apartment in the city, a child in the cradle, fine suits and expensive dresses, and lampshades everywhere.

For eight years fame and money increased. Then Hitler came in, and we left Germany.

We still had our house in Austria, and for five years we were allowed to stay there.

Then our time was up; we had to flee.

We took different and dangerous routes and were reunited in Switzerland. Of our possessions we still had three suits, eight dresses, and two children.

Then followed emigration and immigration and everything that has been described in this book.

To tell about getting reacquainted with Europe would take another book.

I can only say that it was different, quite different from the way we had imagined it.

The cities were more terribly destroyed than we had envisioned in our worst nightmares.

The city-dwellers crept about the streets as if they were parts of the crumbling houses and were put together out of bits of ashes, dust, and rubble. But gradually a bright layer began to appear in the piles of dust. It was like the tender skin that begins to grow over infected wounds. It was a layer of unknown persons, whose presence we had not even suspected. It was material out of which something new could be built.

This layer was composed for the most part of young people who wanted to give their lives form and sense, together with older persons who had decency and character and believed in hope. It was a duty to help this group. It was necessary for their survival and for peace to establish contact between them and the rest of the world.

We found enemies again, too. They were unchanged. A few had been destroyed. Others sit behind bars. Many have assumed straitjackets of denazification to convince people that they are normal again, but they are just waiting for a new era of insanity, when crimes will again be legally permitted and the mentally ill will again achieve power and honor.

We looked for our friends. Many were dead, blown to pieces by bombs, burned up in fires, or hanged by Hitler's courts.

The surviving ones were basically unchanged. But everything was different, quite different from what we had expected.

We experienced success. Zuck's plays appeared in innumerable theaters. Countless letters arrived, many containing real substance.

Success is something very attractive and pleasant, if you know your limitations and practice a becoming modesty.

It makes life easier and it makes it possible to help many others. Sometimes it even has the unusual rewards of real joy and gratitude for your good fortune.

Everything began again for us, as if the thirteen years of murder, plague, and death had not interrupted our lives.

Once during a discussion with twelve hundred students in a packed university hall, Zuck was asked, "You say that you found your homeland in America. How is that possible?"

Yes—how is that possible?

In an American book I once found the sentence: "Everyone loves his native land, whether he was born there or not."

We have a good life in Europe.

We have suffered no real disappointments, for if you accept people and things as they are you cannot be disappointed.

We live most of the time in Switzerland near Lake Geneva.

We have spent summers in Saas-Fee, a village by a glacier at an elevation of six thousand feet, separated from Zermatt and the Matterhorn by high mountains.

We have our own little apartment there, three rooms, a kitchen with an electric stove, and a bathroom.

Zuck has written a new play there. I have been able to cook and bake again, and the housework is so little trouble that I have had time to work on this book. From the windows of our apartment we can see fourteen peaks that are over twelve thousand feet high, with glaciers, larch woods, meadows, and fields, one of the most beautiful and grand landscapes in the world.

We are staying in Saas–Fee until the beginning of winter.

The summer visitors are long gone, and the autumn work on the farms is beginning.

In the Wallis you can find rye, oats, barley, potatoes, and vegetable gardens up to an elevation of six thousand feet. They are beginning to thresh in the cottages that stand on stone feet like our corncrib in Barnard. Potatoes and late vegetables are being brought in. Manure is being spread on the fields. It is time to butcher the pigs and sheep, and one night foxes came into the village, howling and baying at the moon as they looked for the blood and entrails of the butchered animals whose cut-up carcasses hung along the barn walls in the moonlight.

We live in the most beautiful parts of Switzerland. Sometimes we go to Germany, sometimes to Austria.

But, wherever we go, we are visitors and never at home.

It is that way in Saas–Fee.

I like the landscape, the apartment, and the people who own the apartment. They are carpenters and mountain guides, and in their simplicity and independence they remind me of our Barnard neighbors.

I like the ease of my housework, and I listen with joy to Zuck's typewriter. It sounds like a mill that can hardly take care of the quantity of grain given to it.

But this is when and where I first began to have a waking dream that has returned again and again. It is a brother of Drude, but is her opposite in being a daydream of wish fulfillment. My dream is that I am on a journey to America. I board a ship in Rotterdam, one of the slow ships, for I want to recover the time, night after night, that I lost on the journey to Europe.

Finally I arrive in Hoboken and go from there directly to New York.

I have many friends there, but I go first to those who seem to me most "American." I like them, trust them, feel that I can

205

place my fate in their hands. I can accept much from them without feeling oppressed by a sense of obligation. Between us there is passionate objectivity, respectful dignity, and affectionate coolness.

The next night I am already on my way from Grand Central to the junction town, where I arrive the next morning.

That town has not become more beautiful in my absence. I go to my Swiss hotel owners and tell them about Switzerland, but what I really want is to hear the latest news from them. How is the hotel doing? What's new with the help? Have they had any trouble with drunkenness? How are things across the river in the university town?

Then I take the bus to my town, for I still have to get myself a new car again. I travel a stretch of road that I have gone over a hundred times before, but now I am aware, as if for the first time, of the distance and of the straight, unbending sky over the landscape.

We arrive in the town, where I unload my luggage and go first of all to our landlord's store.

It smells of chocolate, apples, and iron tools. I say, "Hello," and the landlord answers, "Hello," and everything is the way it was.

I go into other stores. They greet me and say, "Back again?" as if I had gone away only a week ago. No one says, "Hello, stranger," because they only use that expression when people have been away for a short time, or have perhaps been prevented from coming into the store for three or four weeks by a snowstorm or similar catastrophe.

I go to the snack bar to get a quick cup of coffee and something to eat.

It smells of vanilla, ice, beer, toothpaste, coffee, celery, fried meat, and woodcutters' jackets.

A boy about seventeen years old is resting his head sentimentally on his hand as he sings to his girl, accompanied by the juke box from which he has conjured up the latest hit with his nickel. His elbow rests dreamily on a pile of rolls of toilet paper, stacked up next to the counter for clearance this week.

I can't explain why I delight in all this. Later I go over to the gift shop, where it smells of lavender, candles, and herbs.

She is still there, the old lady who sells the lovely things:

206

fabrics, purses, post cards, cups, and little boxes. I feel like apologizing for buying and taking her things away, for each is a part of the world that surrounds her, and it seems important to preserve her surroundings unchanged.

Next door is a store that has everything from almonds to nails and is like a Lübeck department store. When you enter the store you automatically lower your voice because it is solemn inside like a church. The salespeople are businesslike, but fair, and ready to let you have some of the wonderful variety that the store contains.

Then there are the jolly stores of the town, in which you buy meat and vegetables, and where you have to be ready for puns, jokes, satire, and irony.

There is a big store, part of a chain of stores that goes across the whole country.

The manager sees me as I come in and waves, but I quietly wait my turn to speak to him. Pushing ahead is not acceptable, even for reunions.

There is the clothing store. It is bigger and finer than it was, and it has neon lights and a new sign, but the owners are the same.

I go to the post office, where we shake hands. They tell me that one of them has retired after twenty-four years of service.

I go to the mill, where I have always bought feed for our animals and coal for our stoves. I say "Hello" and that I will soon need feed and coal again.

Finally I drive to the farm, taking the long way through the village. I stop at the post office and ask if there is any mail for us, and receive letters and flyers that have waited for us there for two years.

The postmistress says, ". . . probably glad to be back," and I nod.

Then I drive down the steep road through the woods and turn sharply into the dirt road to our house.

At this point Zuck appears, suddenly sitting beside me in the car.

I have to shift into low gear. It is summer, but the steep road has many bumps, and it looks as if it has just rained. We drive through the enchanted wood, past the lynx rock. Then comes the meadow, and there is the house.

We open the door and stand in the kitchen.

We set our suitcases on the floor, put away the things I have bought, and are home.

Zuck will build a fire in the big fireplace and we will sit in front of it and plan.

We have to realize first that we are in the strange situation of earning money in Europe in order to live in America, a reversal of historical tradition. But we have to plan carefully and be sure that we are starting out correctly. Success and money will probably come in America, too, but we cannot count on it.

We are going to find a new way, a new schedule. We are going to manage the daily work so that it leaves Zuck time to write.

The chairs on which we are sitting must have new covers, and the living room curtains are getting shabby and faded.

There is much to do, but we know what we are dealing with, and this time we won't let the work get the better of us.

That is how I imagine my journey to America. Even dreams of America are real, right into all the details of everyday life.

My America has no place for sentimental gratitude. It has no numbness of habit, no tradition, no memory, even none of the feeling that a woman might have who has left home to follow her foreign-born husband to his homeland.

But there is something else, a factor which we had never before encountered. That is the experience of a "native land," a place in which one is reborn through a second childhood.

In America we learned anew to walk, listen, touch, smell, and taste. Of course we could not speak the language correctly and had a foreign accent, but people understood us, and we knew what they were saying.

In writing this book in German, I have had the grotesque difficulty that I knew hardly a word that had to do with barns, animals, or tools in my native language, for I had never learned the vocabulary of everyday living in Europe.

The dream of returning to America, of longing to go home, has nothing to do with the past.

I am in the present when I smell the wood fire in our fireplace, when I see the air shimmer over the pond, when I watch the northern lights in the night sky.

208

I smell coffee, bacon, eggs, and warm bread in the morning. I hear the animals in the distance, and the stillness nearby, and everything is alive, as in the days of childhood.

The ties to the new land are as strong as if we had always lived there.

We have many ties to Europe. To cut them would be foolish, selfish, and wanton.

The difference between the two worlds is enormous. Going to Europe is called in America "going abroad," an expression that the thesaurus equates with "distant suns, Ultima Thule, no one knows where, and the end of the world."

"Everyone loves his native land, whether he was born there or not."

It is a many-sided homesickness, the deep longing that we have for our new land. It is a feeling for the present that holds future in every action. It is a simple love for everyday living.

THE END

Epilogue

(Translators' note: Alice Herdan-Zuckmayer wrote two different endings for The Farm in the Green Mountains. *The first, which begins on page 205, was part of the original book, published in 1949 — before the Zuckmayers returned to America. The second, which follows, was written nineteen years later.)*

We had been in Europe for five years, in Germany, in Austria, in Switzerland, but wherever we went we were visitors and never at home. The apartment we had had in Berlin had been completely destroyed by bombs.

The confiscated house in Austria had been given back to us, but the damage that the house had suffered in the nine years of our absence seemed too great to be worth the money and effort to put it back in good condition. Also, everything had changed. There were new buildings around our house, and the place was no longer the village with large farms and fields we remembered, but had become a suburb of Salzburg. So we sold the house we had won back.

And after five years we set out on the journey back to America, back to the farm.

The farm did not belong to us, but its owner, our Mr. Ward, had taken care of it and kept it for us. During the summers he had rented it to unusually nice people from the city, and in the winters he had packed and wrapped up the little house to withstand snow, ice, and storms.

We sailed on a slow ship, and I enjoyed winning back the

time, night after night, that I had lost on the journey to Europe. On five different evenings the notice appeared on the blackboard: "Today at midnight the clock will be set back one hour." This time we arrived, not in Hoboken, but at a pier in New York. Zuck had to take care of business, and I went in search of friends. I went first to those who seemed to me most "American." Between us there was passionate objectivity, respectful dignity, and affectionate coolness. There was not much questioning, investigating, or probing, as in Europe. I did not have to do much explaining and found an understanding that comprehended diverse feelings and points of view.

A week later, at midnight, we were on our way from Grand Central Station to Vermont.

We traveled in a comfortable sleeping car, which we had all to ourselves, including a small private washroom. The wide bunks were soft, and we could have slept well if we had not been almost thrown out of bed by the terrible rattling and shaking of the car and the sudden stopping of the train.

The railroads, cars and tracks, had deteriorated in our absence and were in a truly deplorable state. So we sat pressed against the walls of the bunks, hanging on to the chrome bars on the wall and watching our luggage tumble down, just missing us, to the floor, where it jumped and rolled about.

After we had been traveling for about three hours, it was suddenly deathly quiet. The train had stopped at a station, and there it stood for three hours waiting for a couple of cars from another train that it had to take to Canada. Suddenly we remembered that the night train had always acted in this puzzling and senseless way. So we loosened our grip on the bars and fell sound asleep. Three hours later we were rudely shaken awake. We sat up because it was better to be pushed about in a sitting position than tossed up and down like a football while lying down. A few hours later we actually arrived, and the train was still on the track.

Not many years after this, that railroad line was discontinued.

We arrived at the junction point. The station and the town had not grown more beautiful, but on the platform was standing one of our dearest friends, and near him a large truck to take our luggage. We embraced and our cheeks became very wet, but the warm sun dried them.

First we all drove in the truck to our shopping center, the little town with beautiful old houses and many stores. The two men sat down in the snack bar and drank beer. I did errands the way I always had.

First of all I went to the store that belonged to our landlord. It smelled of chocolate, cheese, and iron tools. The owner's sister was there. She pressed my hands and said, "Joe is up on the farm. He is expecting you."

Then I looked in quickly at the shop of the old lady who sold the lovely things: fabrics, purses, aprons, toys, cups, plates, and glasses. I looked for a big old-fashioned kitchen apron, something that was not so easy to find among the new styles of maid's aprons and fig leaves. The lady was elegant and very old, almost ninety. But she recognized me and called me by name. "How good to see you back," she said. Then she tripped over to the counter, bent her white head to hide her emotions, picked a little white and green pillow out of the things there, and laid it in my hands. It was filled with balsam pine needles and was fragrant. I thanked her for the unexpected gift and placed it with the apron in my purse. Then I went next door, into the fine, large store that carries everything from stone-ground flour to caviar, from almonds to nails of all sizes and kinds. When I entered that store I automatically lowered my voice because it was so quiet and solemn inside. The sales-persons had always been reserved, but quietly ready to find what I wanted from the wonderful variety and get it for me.

I found Zuck there in the coffee section, and our friend by the wines, where he was looking over the bottles and making his selection.

The owner and the clerks came over and greeted us as if we had been away only a week.

But then the storm broke.

It was in the grocery store, where we buy meat, vegetables, and fruit, and where it is noisy and cheerful like a market-place. There people ran up to us, hugged us, kissed us, shook our hands practically out of their sockets, and showed in their joy at seeing us again not a trace of New England reserve.

We were quite overcome, and our friend rescued us into his car and drove us up to his wonderful, old house on the hill.

212

We sit the way we had in former times at his beautifully set dinner table. The man of the house carves the roast and distributes the slices. His wife fills the plates with vegetables and rice. The children sit in their usual places, but now they are grown up.

The man of the house says, "I thank God that our friends have returned home."

Soon we had to break away to get home.

The two men sat up front in the cab, and I settled down on the luggage. We drove to the farm, with a detour through Barnard. That is the stretch of road that I have gone over a hundred times before, but now I am aware of the distance and of the straight, unbending sky over the landscape. We still had the reunion with the people of Barnard, a torrent so fed by springs of affection and joy that we were almost borne along on its current.

We drive on from Barnard, down the road, and then turn sharply left into the woods. We have to shift into low gear because the woods road is just the same — steep, bumpy, and narrow. We drive through the enchanted wood, past the lynx rock. Then comes the meadow, on the other side the pond, and there is the house.

The barn door is open, and our Mr. Ward is working in the barn.

The luggage is unloaded. Mr. Ward helps me carry the groceries into the kitchen, and I put away the things I have bought.

Mr. Ward says that the electric stove isn't working.

Zuck gets wood and makes a fire in the kitchen stove.

Our friend says goodbye and takes Mr. Ward back with him to town. Evening falls and it is frosty, but the old iron stove warms us. . . .

It is now nineteen years since I finished writing this book. The book ended with a dream, a waking dream of returning to the farm that came back again and again. The dream has become reality, and this reality surpassed all my dream images.

In this first summer we got back some of the animals that we had left with a farmer: three goats, six laying hens, our ducks Goesta and Emma, and above all our wolfhound Bertram. So the sheds, the meadows, and the pond were full of life, and there was a little milking and feeding to take care of.

Everything should have been just the way it had been, but we had changed. We had become unaccustomed to work, and even the small amount of work gave us trouble. We were no longer used to having to interrupt every piece of intellectual work, whether it was writing or reading, to feed animals, chop wood, tend fires, carry heavy water buckets. I even found the housework in the big house too much for me with only a couple of hours a week of hired help.

We began to feel short of time in everything we did, and we were no longer willing to waste time on work that was now not absolutely necessary for survival, as it had been. It was a mild summer, and sometimes I could drive our newly purchased car, a powerful Willis Overland, to the library. There everything was unchanged.

In November we had to return to Europe.

We gave the animals to the farmer, and together with Mr. Ward we packed up the house for winter.

We went back, over there.

Going to Europe the Americans call going "over there," and in the thesaurus I found under "over there" and "abroad" the expressions: distant suns — Ultima Thule — no one knows where — the end of the world.

We didn't return until fall the next year. Our American friends had rented a house for us in the town where we always did our shopping. The house was a hundred years old, but very comfortably furnished. It was on a river, near a high bridge.

In the middle of the town is a park with mighty elms. Birds sing in the quiet side streets where autos stand like patient house animals in front of the houses of their owners or in their yards. There are many people in the town who know the birds not only by their plumage but by their songs.

In the evening, when it gets dark, the people living in the houses do not draw their curtains. Behind the large glass windows stands a table with a bright lamp, and around the table they sit in armchairs knitting or reading. They don't worry about passersby, and the passersby don't watch them through the windows.

The work in the little house on the river was no trouble, and

214

I did not have to be afraid when Zuck was away and I was alone in the house.

In 1953 we were all at the farm. Our older daughter was there with her husband and two children. The younger daughter came to say goodbye, since she had decided to work and live in Germany—later in Austria.

This summer we lived without chickens, goats, and ducks. Our dog had died at the ripe old age of thirteen years.

We had been given a hunting dog and a dachshund puppy.

It would have been a beautiful summer if the shadow of final departure had not hung over it.

After the children had left and we walked about the autumn farm, we knew: everything was different, quite different from the way we had pictured it. We established the fact that we were in the unusual situation of having to earn money in Europe to be able to live in America, a grotesque reversal of historic tradition. We traveled there and here, and here and there, and the traveling and temporary living here and there cost impossible sums.

Many good offers fell through because Zuck again and again had to leave for America at the decisive moment. Everything that had begun in so hopeful and promising a way after our return to Europe seemed to be endangered. Also the American passport requirements then in force became more and more difficult, almost impossible to fulfill, and we slowly began to realize that our existence was threatened.

Success and money would perhaps come some day in America, but we knew then that we couldn't wait for them, that we did not dare to count on them.

The decision was made for us in a strange way. We had no possibility of buying the farm. We could no longer live on it in the winter. We could no longer live with it and in it, and yet we had a many-sided attachment to it. It was a symbol of the most difficult and the happiest time of our life.

In 1955 something happened that we had long expected. The highway came. For years the farmers had fought to keep their land and property, even though they were to receive a large sum of money for the pieces of land that they had to sacrifice to the highway. At first they said that the highway would be built in the valley, far from the farm. Then they said that the highway wouldn't be built at all. But one day it was there, the highway. Right next to the farm, much closer than we had anticipated in our darkest imaginings. Mountains were moved, gorges cut out. The enchanted rocks were destroyed by gigantic machines that stamped and spat through the virgin forest like primeval beasts, cutting off our lonely road through the woods.

The farm is now easy to reach. It lies near the great white highway, and from the pond you can see the shining autos race by.

At the same time plans were being made to encircle the house in Chardonne above Lake Geneva, where for years we had kept a European apartment, with a 180-degree hairpin curve, cutting off pieces from its enchanting garden.

We had spent many summers in Saas-Fee, exactly sixteen between 1938 and 1957. We knew the land and the people.

We often went past a house that was set in a large garden with many trees, and we thought: We would like to live there.

At that time there were not many houses for sale in Saas-Fee.

A few weeks later we signed the purchase papers.

I went back once more to America and gave up the house on the river. I took furniture, books, pictures, and other things we cared about to our new house. For:

"To every thing there is a season, and a time to every purpose under the heaven. A time to be born, and a time to die; a time to plant, and a time to pluck up that which is planted; . . . a time to cast away stones, and a time to gather stones together, a time to embrace, and a time to refrain from embracing; a time to get and a time to lose, a time to keep . . ."